Fairy

Wizard

Minotaur

House Goblin

Ice Queen

Yeti

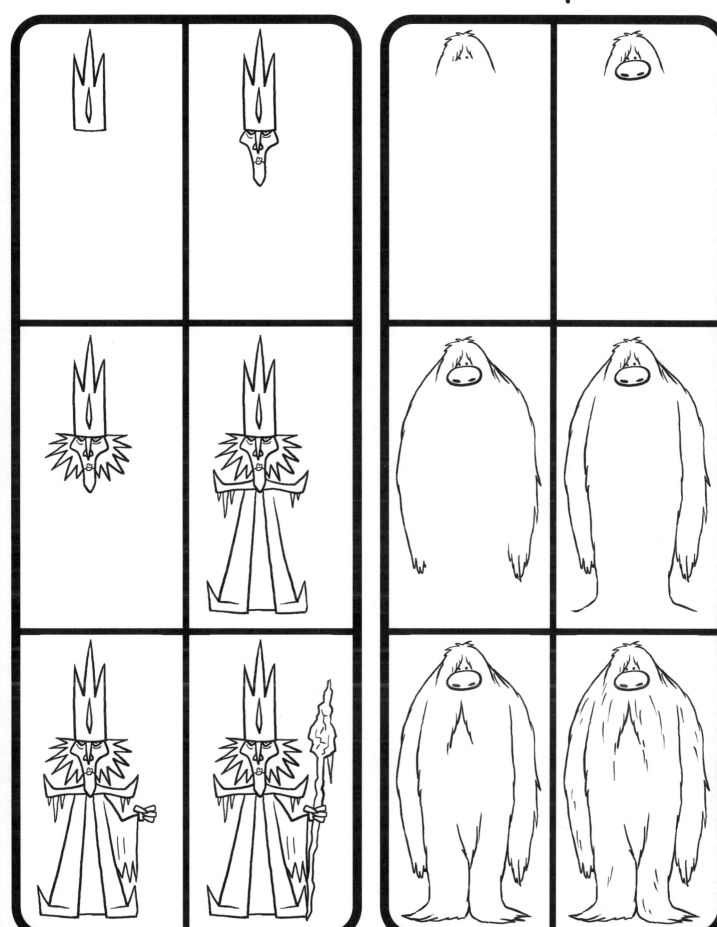

Knight

Dwarf

Witch

Elf King

Phoenix

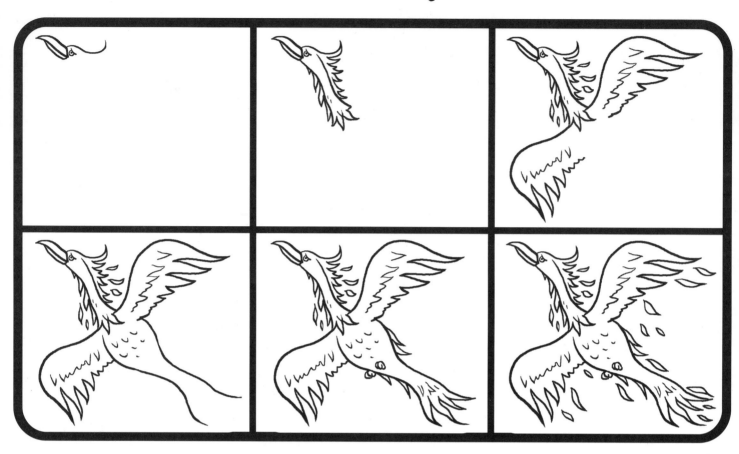

Gremlin

Mermaid

Dragon

Pixie

Zombie

Fairy Queen

Tree Man

Leprechaun

Swamp ogre

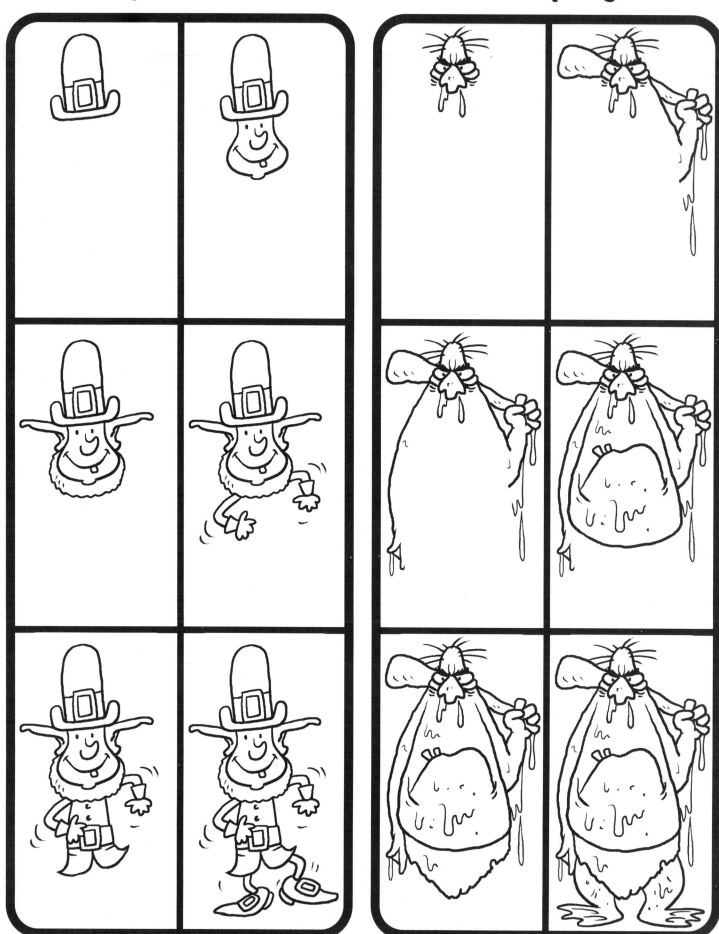

Alien   Nymph

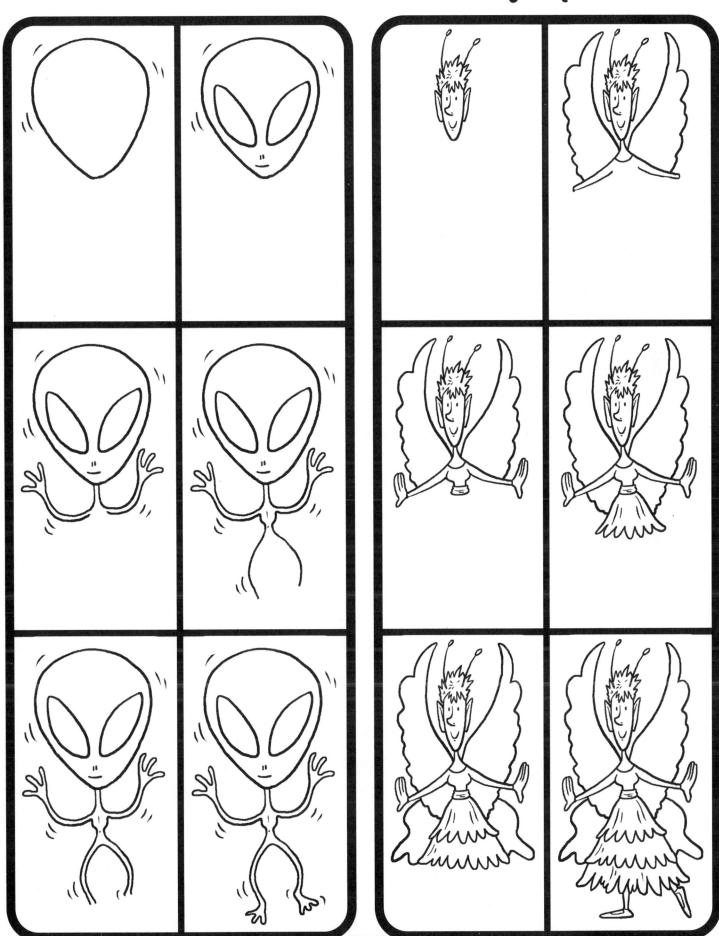

Pegasus

flot Smudger

Two-headed Dog

Giant octopus

Grim Reaper

Prince Charming

Jack frost

Sorceress

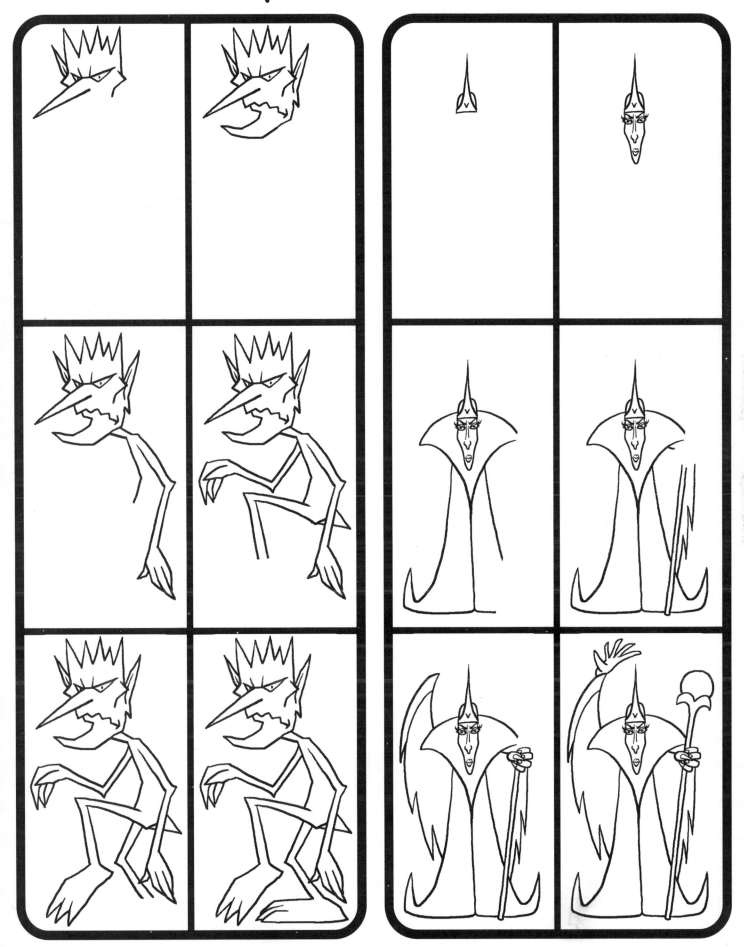

fraggle Snap

Flower fairy

Gnome

Big Bad Wolf

Snotter

Centaur

Thunder Bird

Three-headed ogre

Cave Troll   Dwarf Lady

Elf Queen

Barbarian

Unicorn

King Poseidon

Lesser-spotted Snotter

Giant Worm

Hobgoblin

Tree Lady

Sorcerer

Big foot

Wood Troll

Bogeyman

corn fairy

cyclops

Mug Flump

Will'o'Wisp

Sphinx

Griffin

Lizard Man

Sea Troll

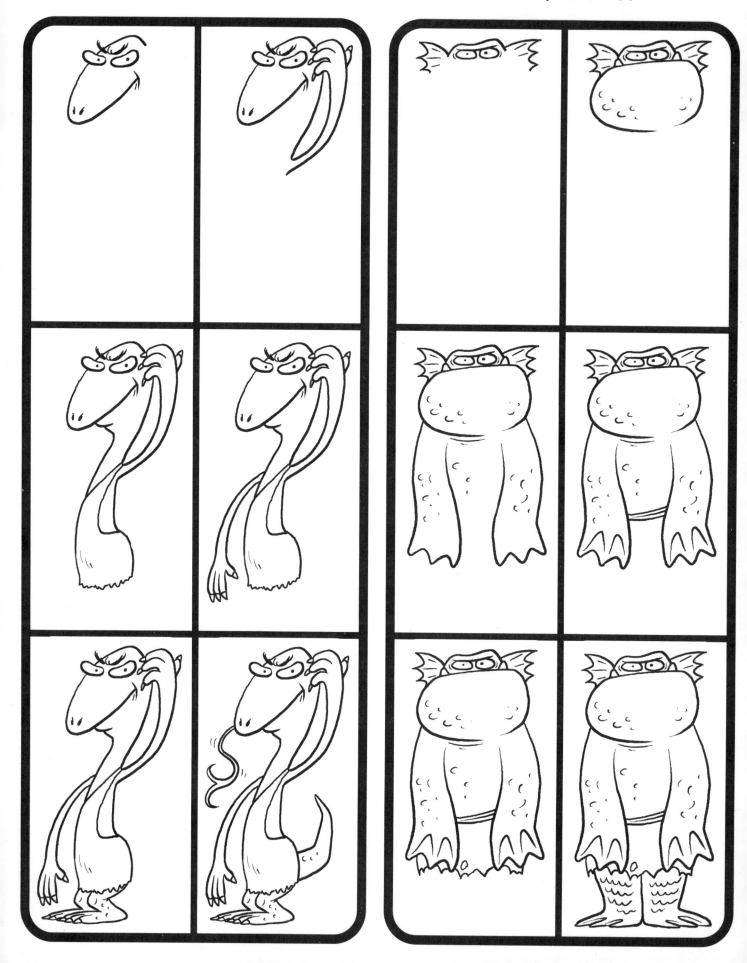

White Witch

Nessie

Fairy King

Unifaun

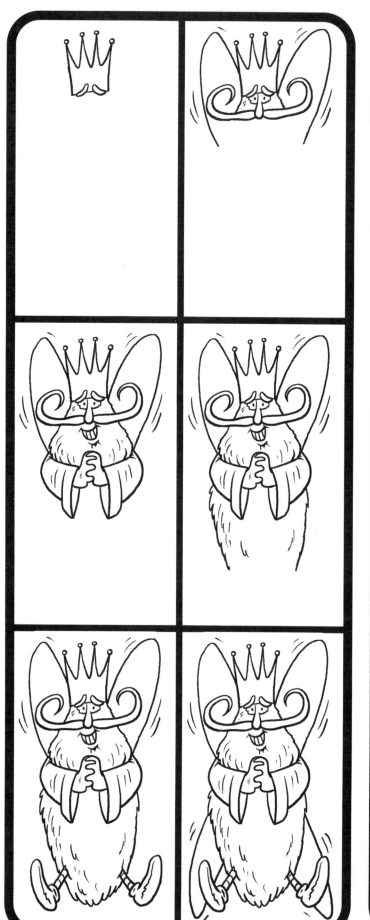

Medusa

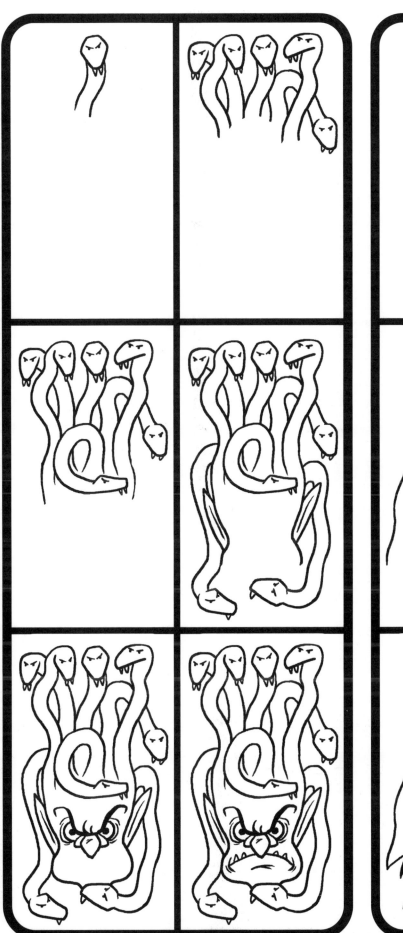

Princess

Harpie

Mushroom Man

Snicker Toad

Giant Spider

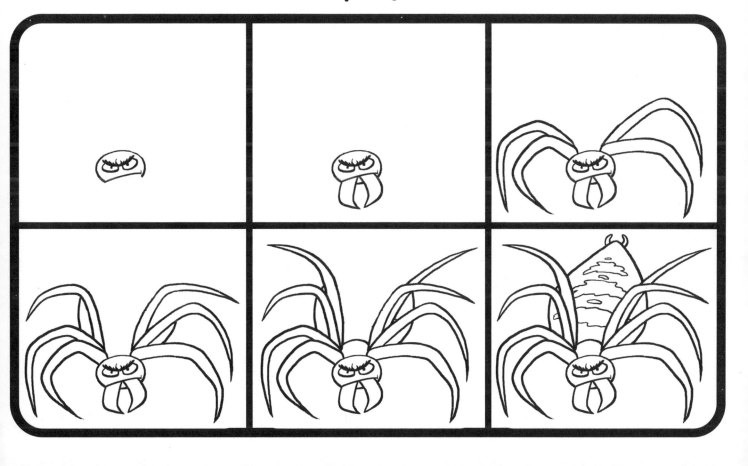

Warlock

Mountain Troll

Sandman

Wood Elf

Jabberwocky

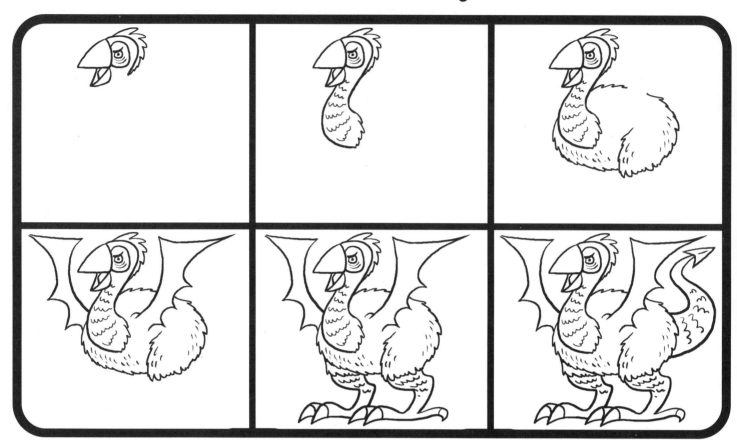

Goat Sucker

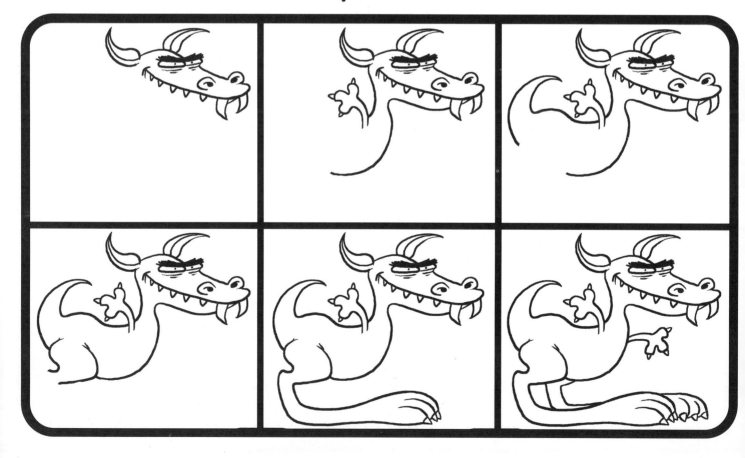

Giant crab

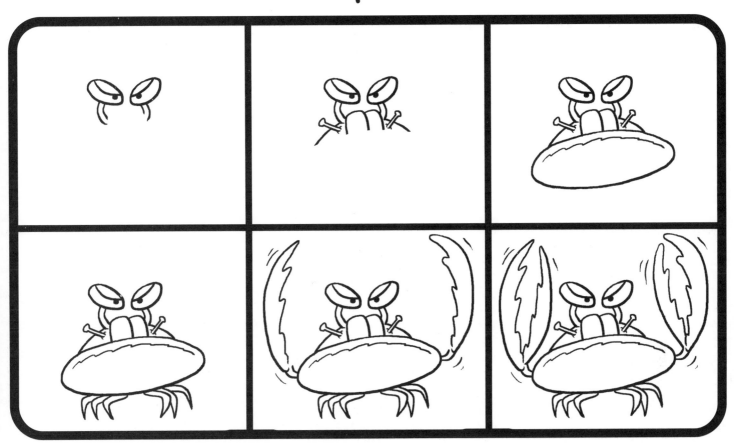

Sprite

Spring-heeled Jack

Siren

Dwarf Lord

Wood Goblin

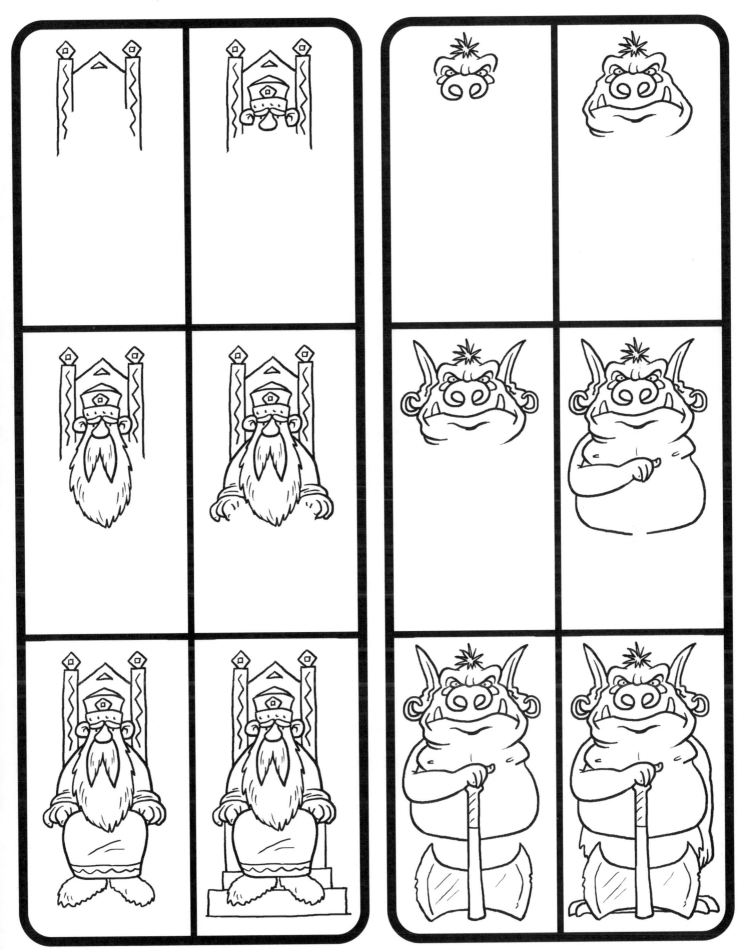

Gargoyle

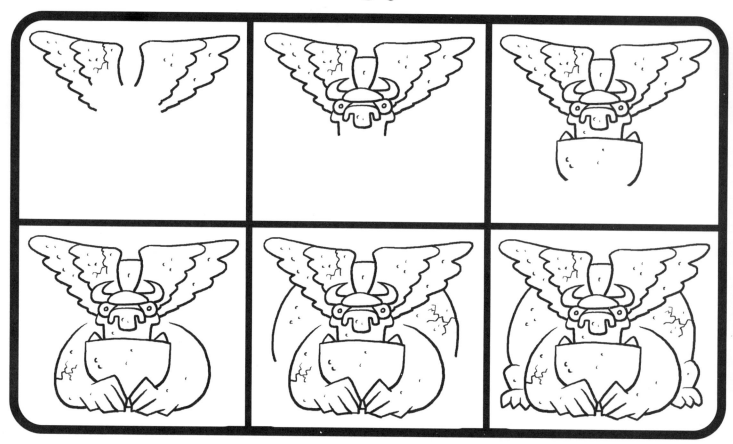

Kraken

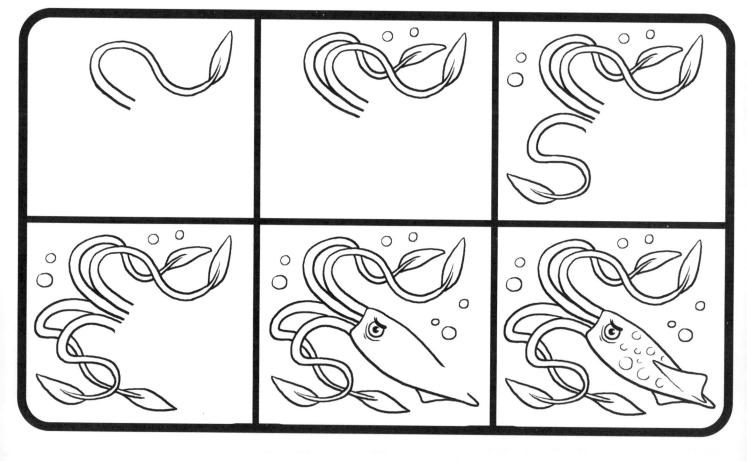

Hippogrif

Bogie

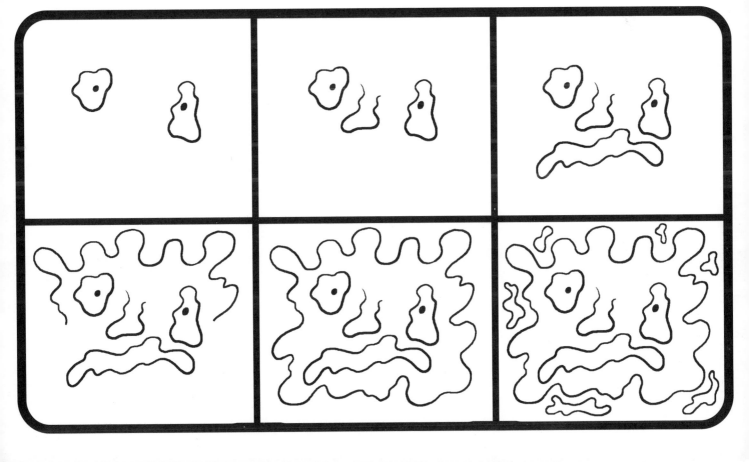

Jub Jub Bird

Cave Goblin

Limey Slop

Borogrove

Shape Changer

Water Nymph

Snarcrack

Earth Titan

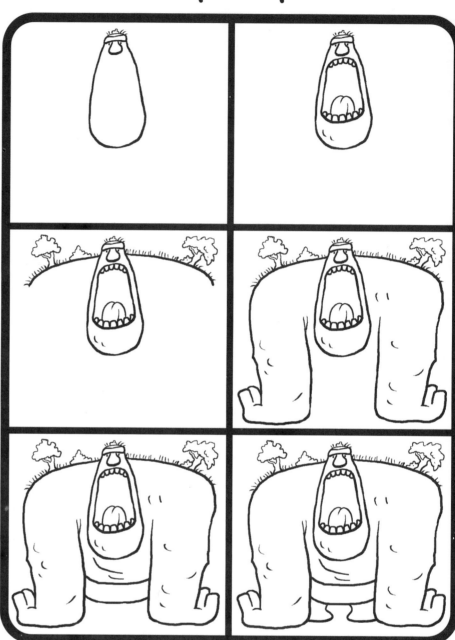

Bander Snatch

Two-headed Snake

Galumph

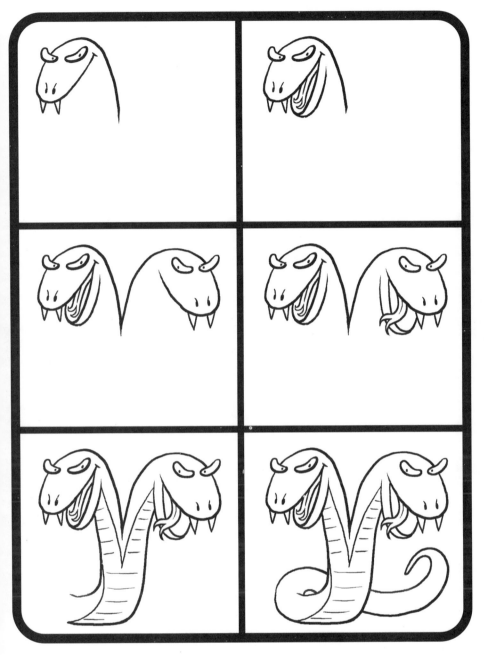

Hades

Tum Tum

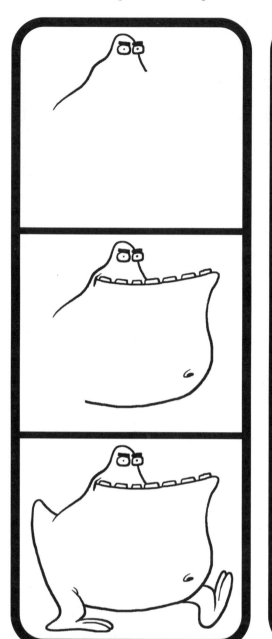

Slithy Tove

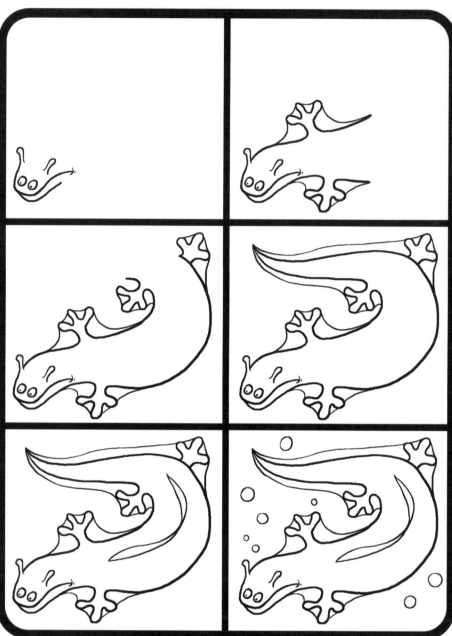

Fire Titan

Bottlenose dolphin

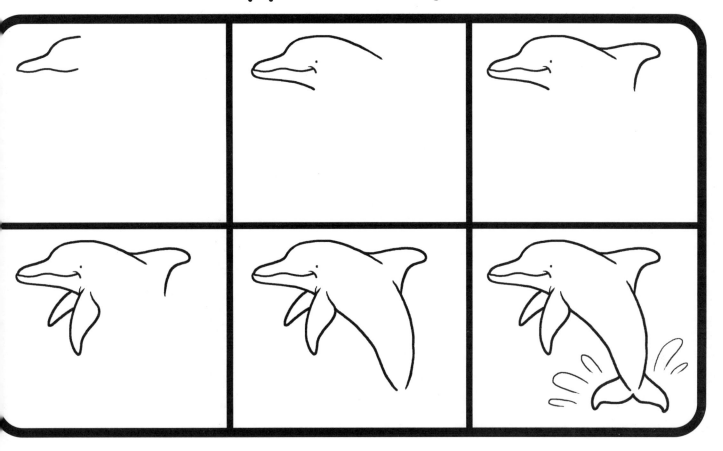

Moorish Idol

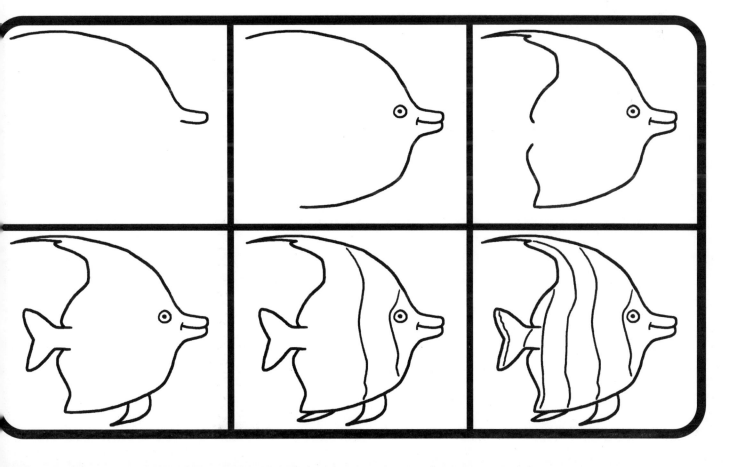

Dolphin fish

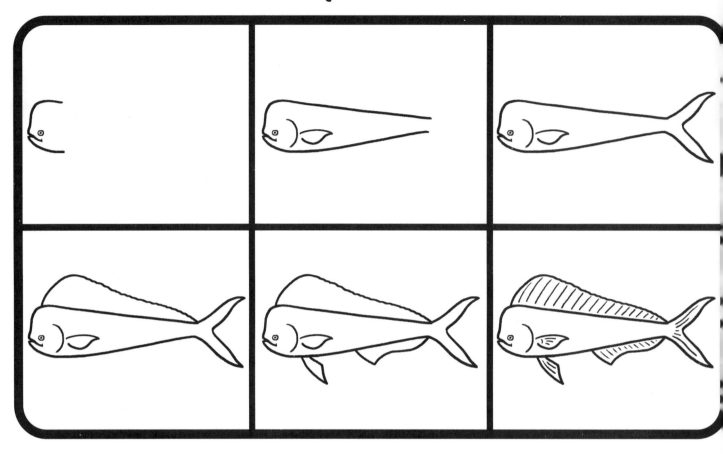

Yellowfin Tuna

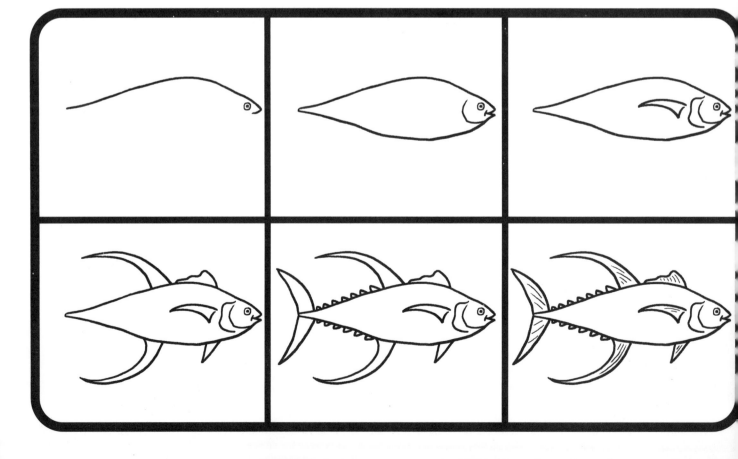

Rockhopper Penguin

Northern Right Whale

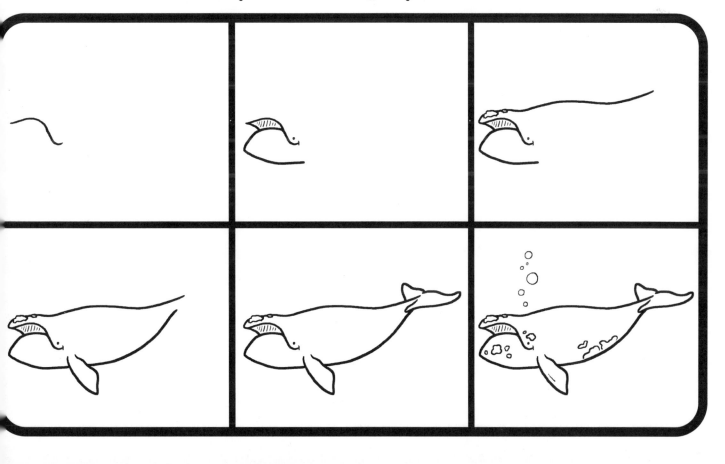

Seahorse

Dolphin and calf

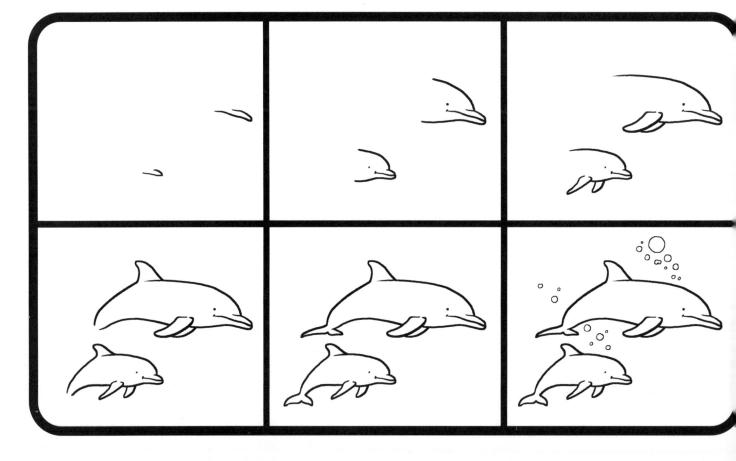

Great White Shark

Yellow Tang

Banded Pipefish

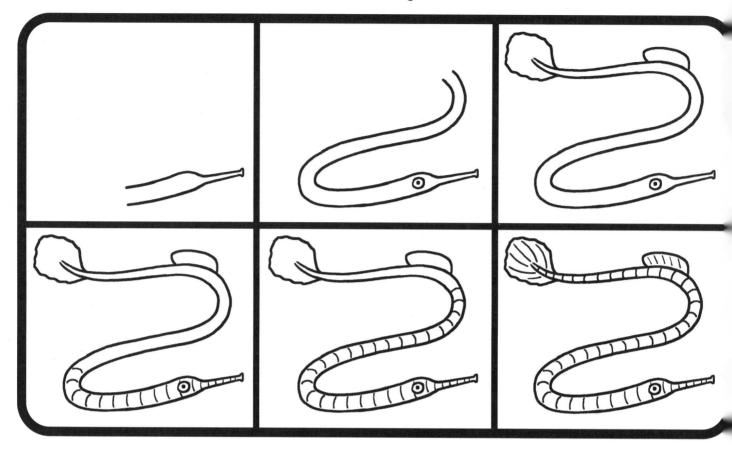

Puffer fish

Shrimp

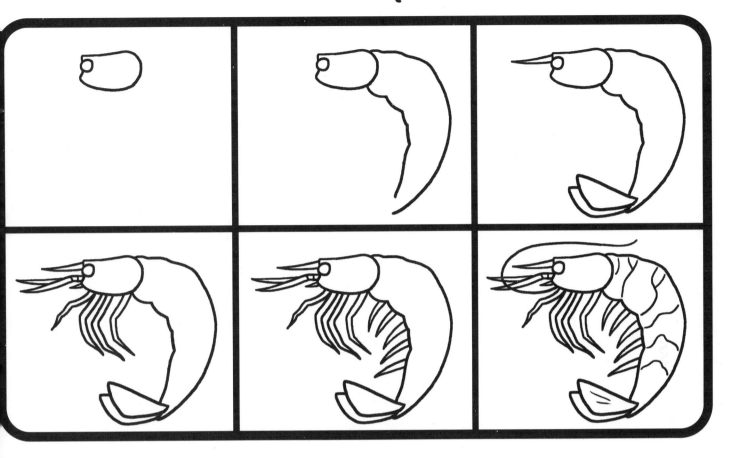

Dugong

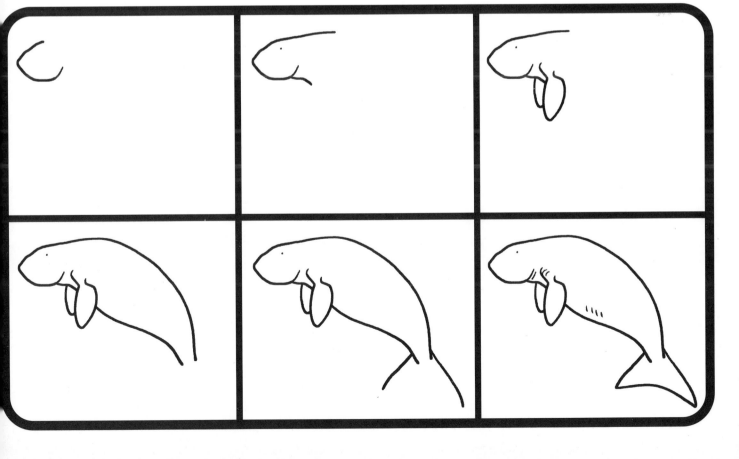

Brown Pelican

Lantern fish

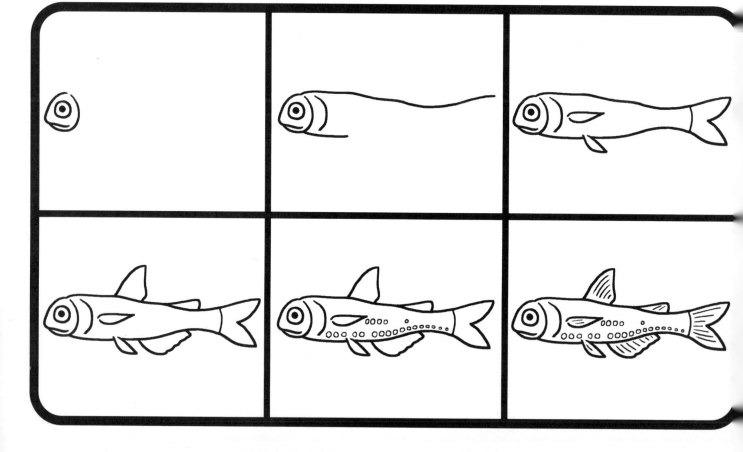

Squid

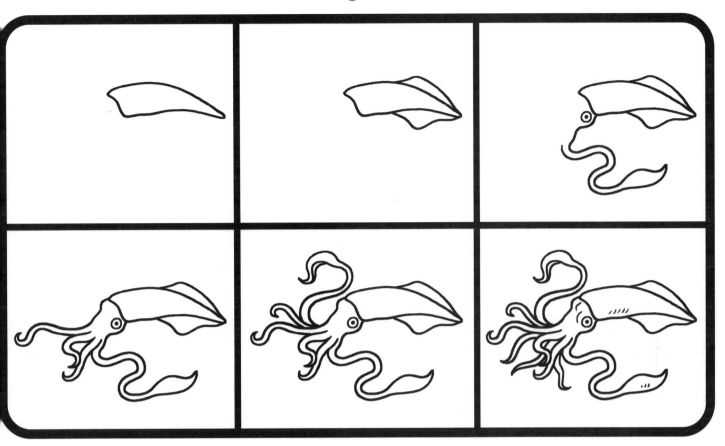

Laughing Dolphin

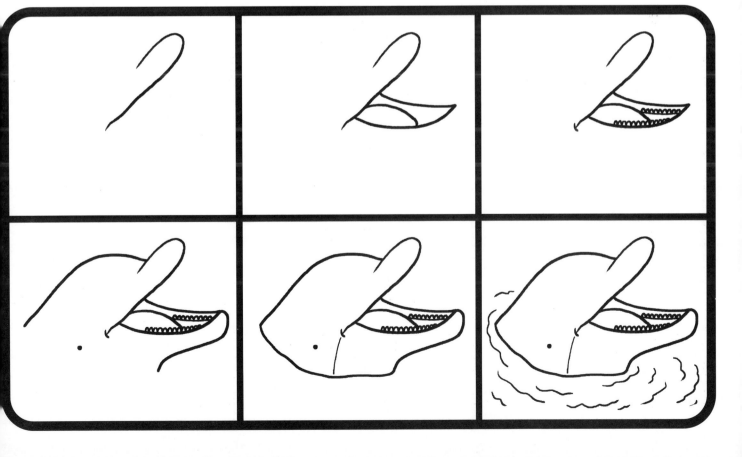

Parrot fish

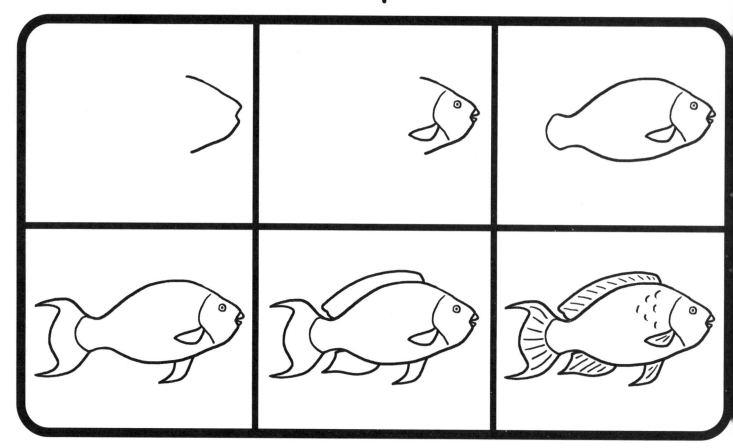

Chinstrap Penguin

Lionfish

Bonnethead Shark

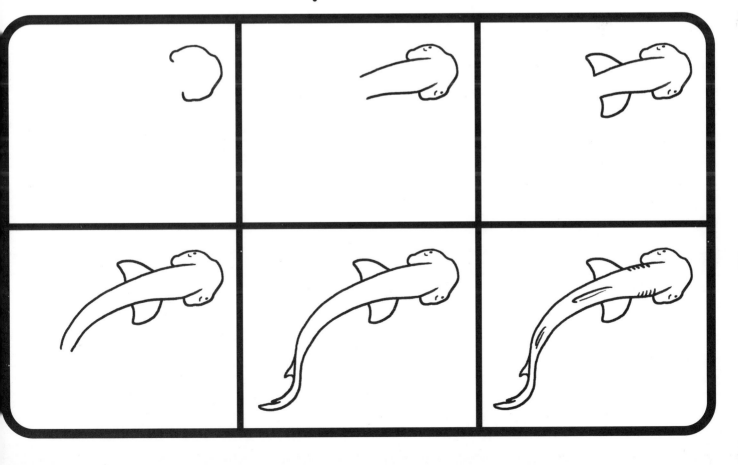

Common Dolphin

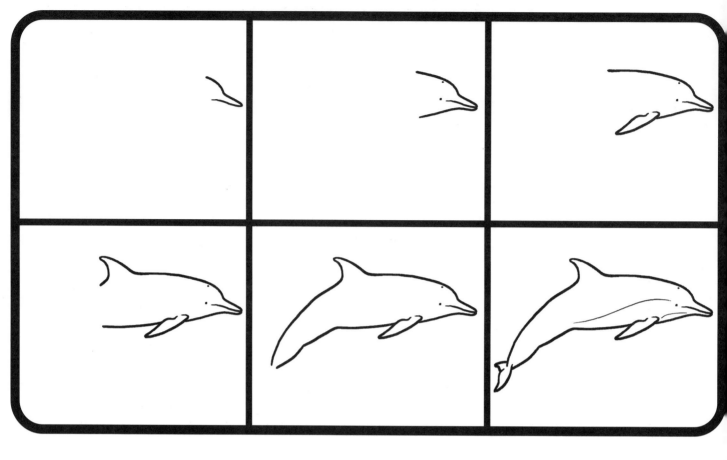

Cod

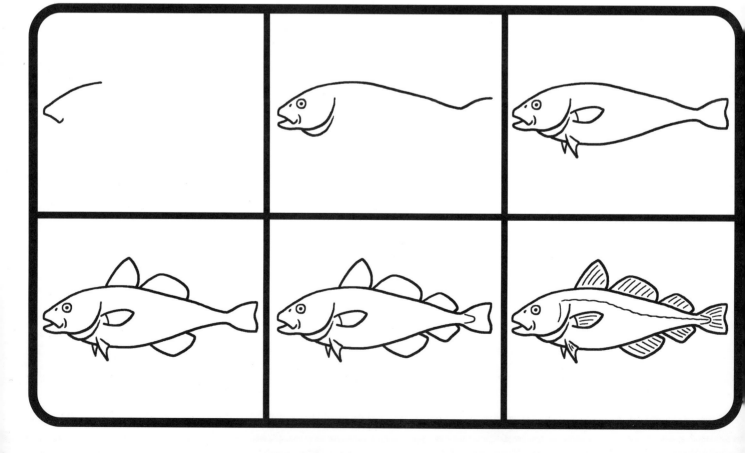

Elephant fish

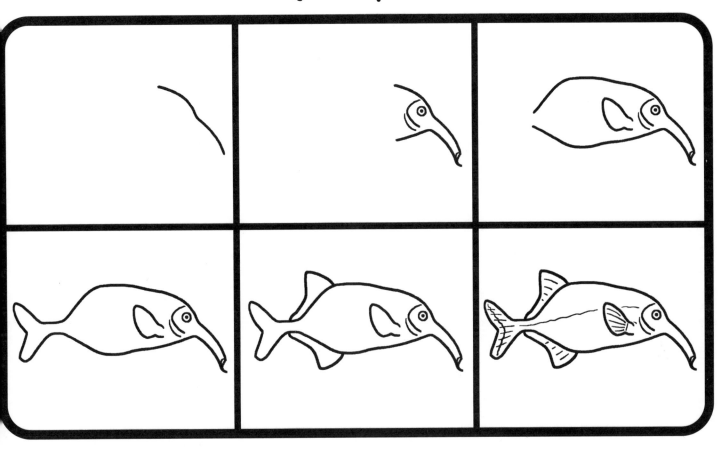

Sperm Whale

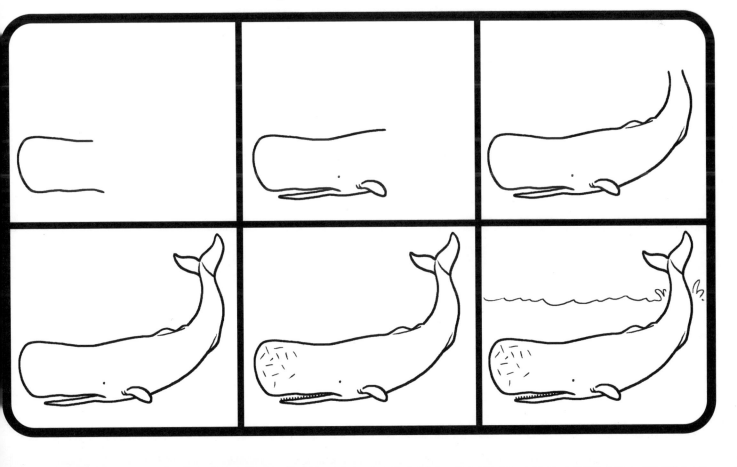

Dolphins playing

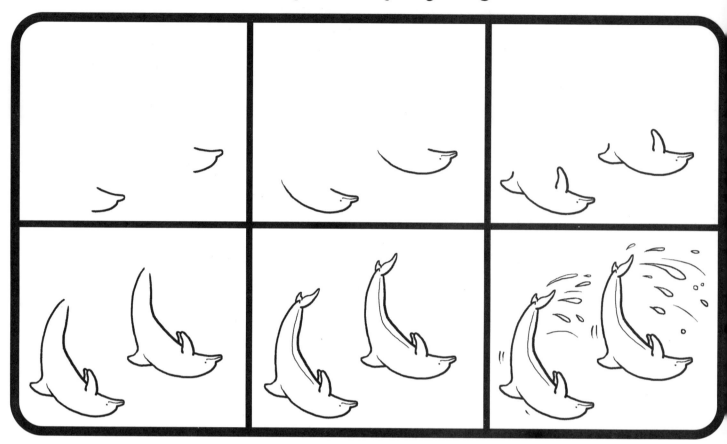

Blue Marlin

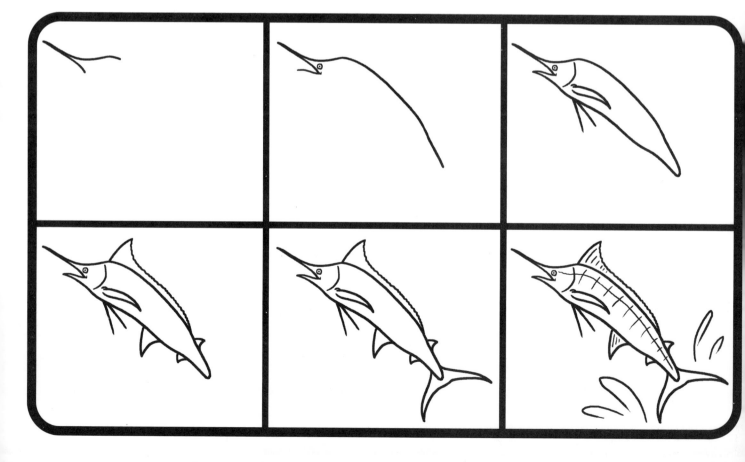

common Puffin

Lobster

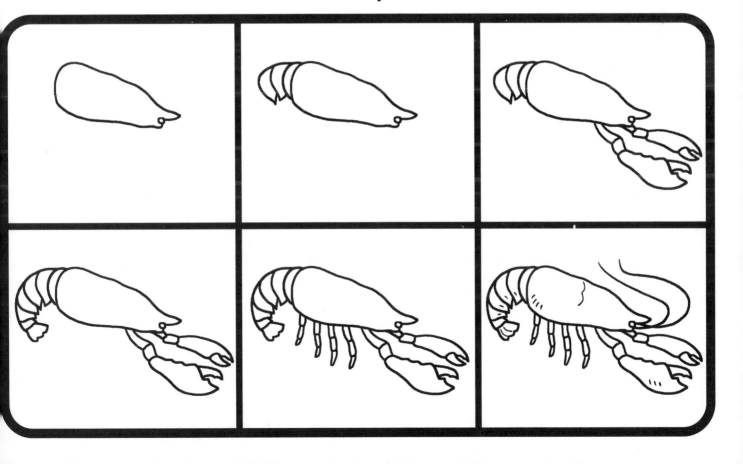

Clownfish

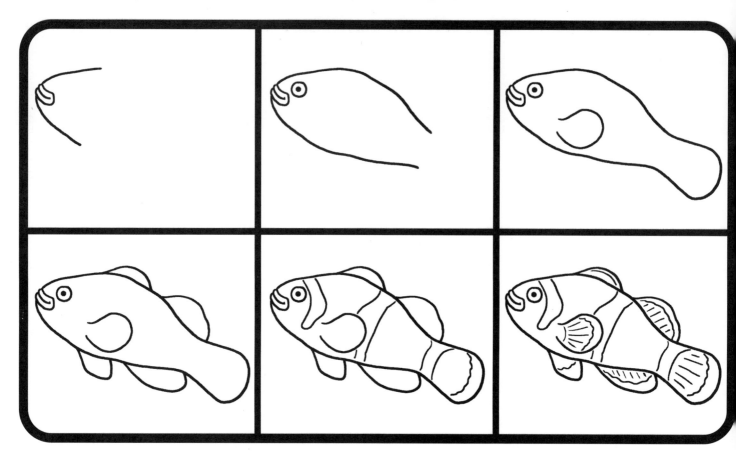

Hammerhead Shark

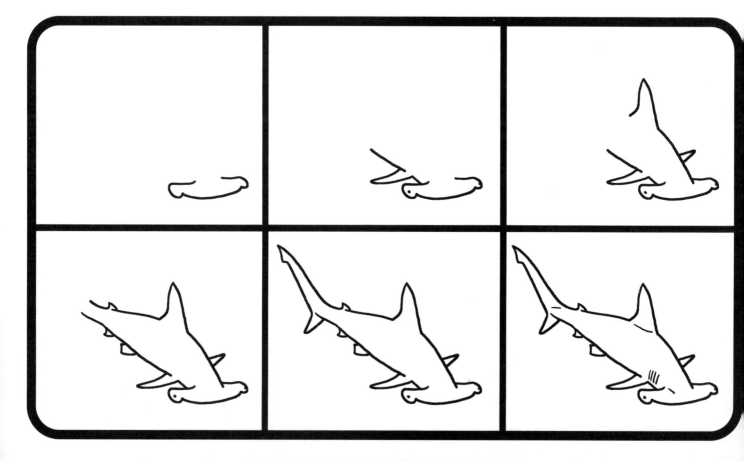

Permit fish

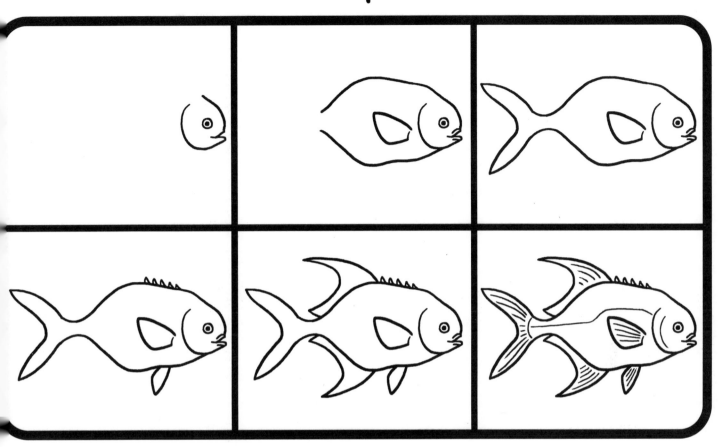

Spotted Dolphin

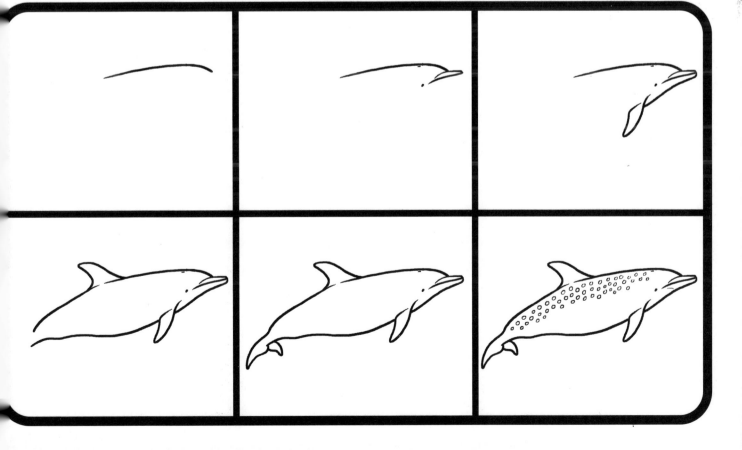

cuttlefish

Pilot Whale

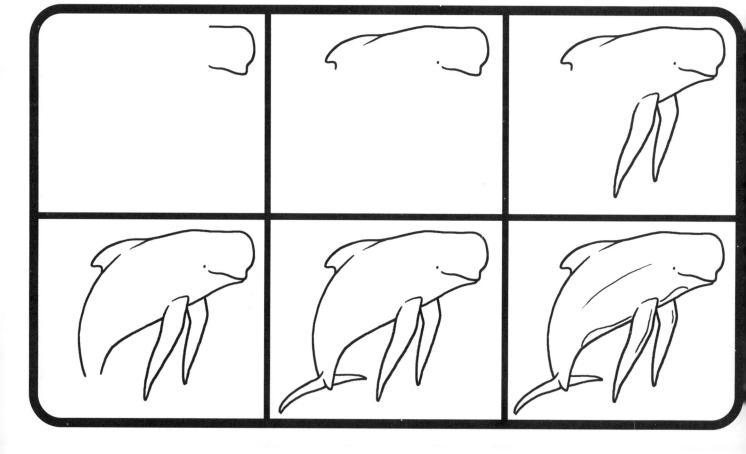

Skate

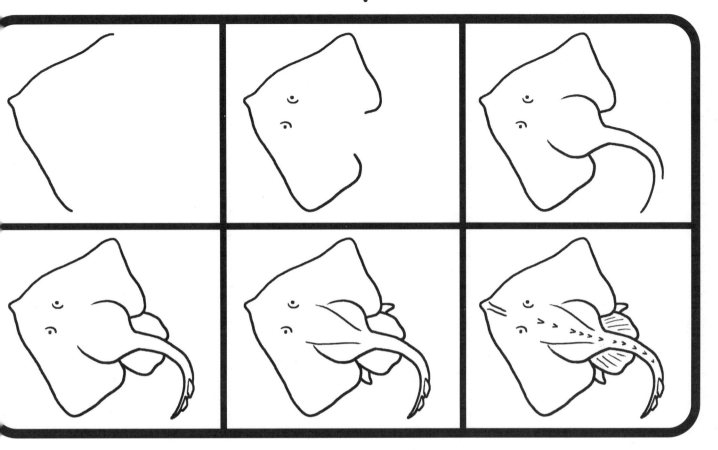

Hermit crab

Blue Whale

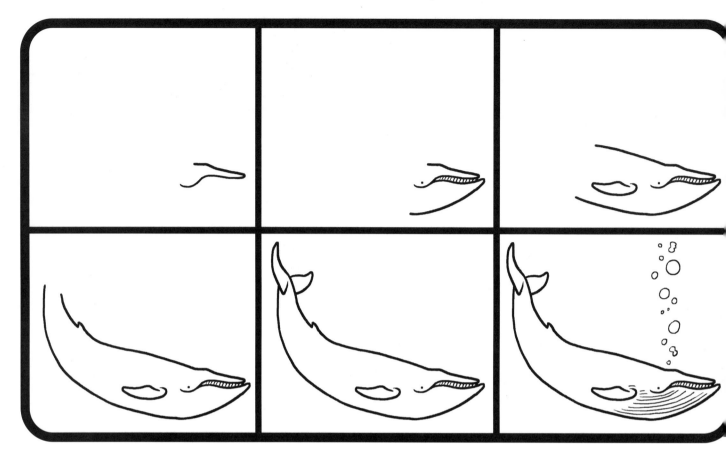

Fire Goby

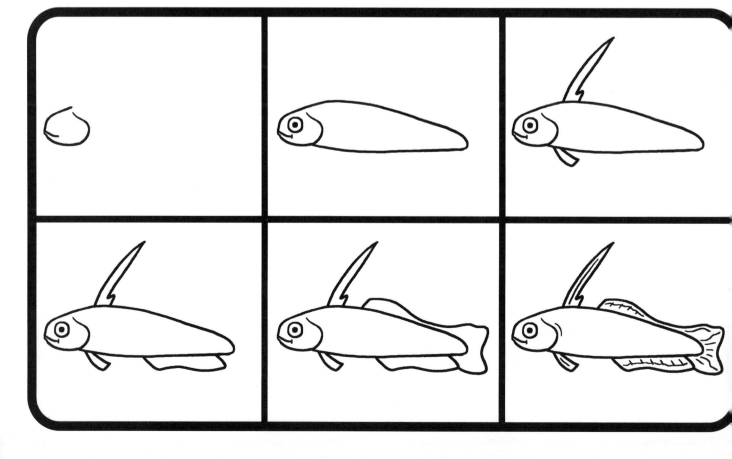

Walrus

Humpback Dolphin

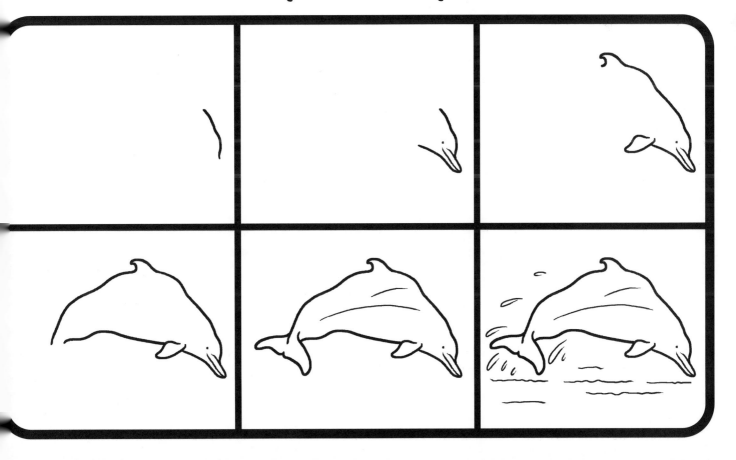

Black Dragonfish

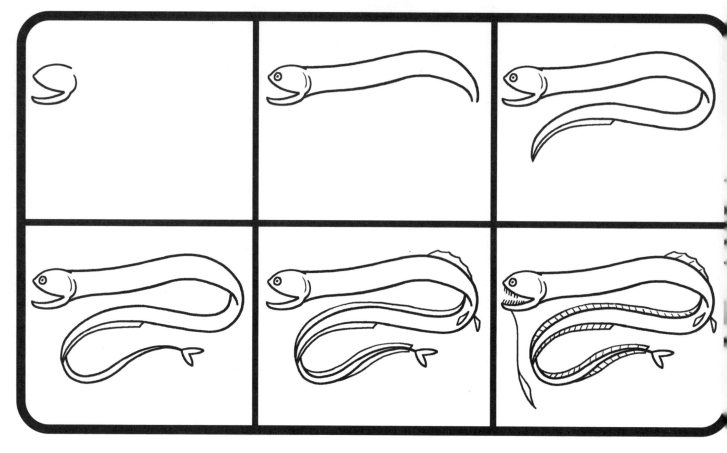

Basking Shark

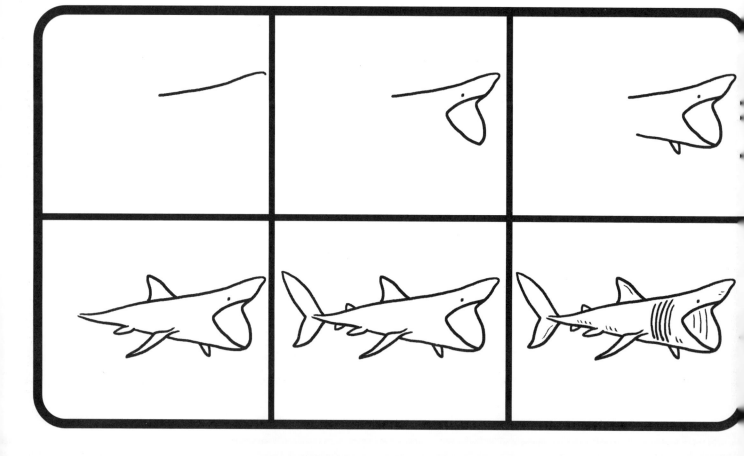

Queen Angelfish

Nautilus

Seagull

Dolphin with ball

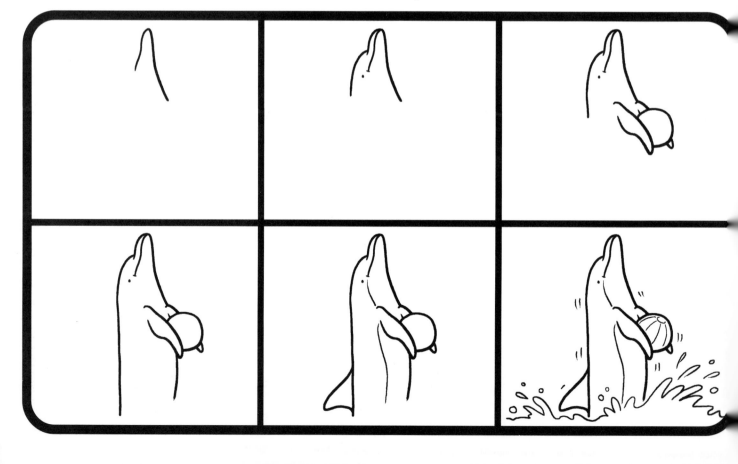

Blue Tang

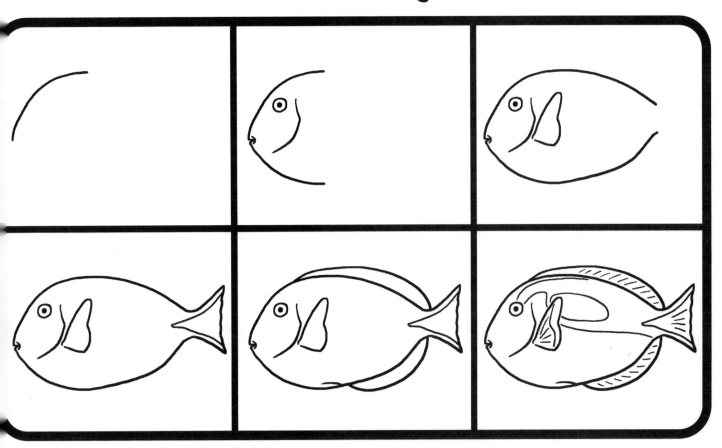

Mandarin fish

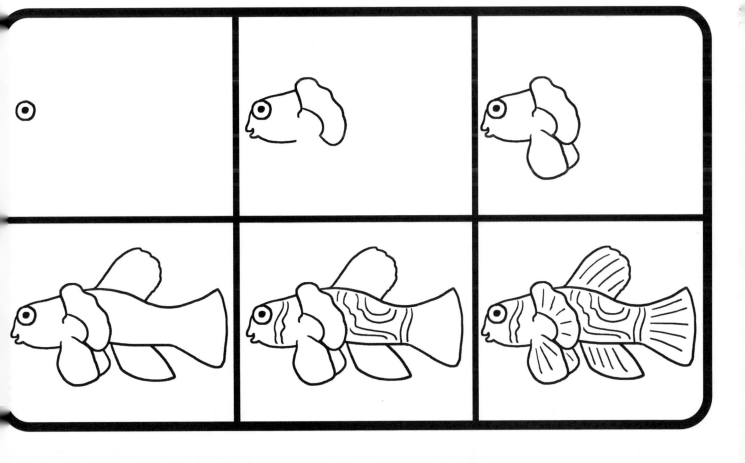

Picasso Triggerfish

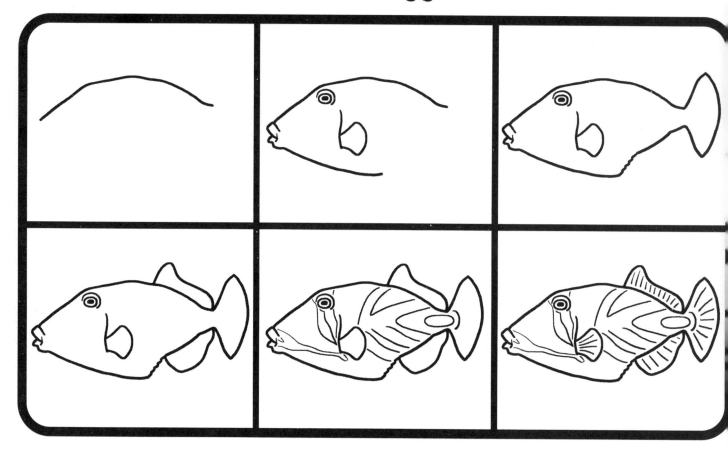

Red Snapper

Emperor Penguin with egg

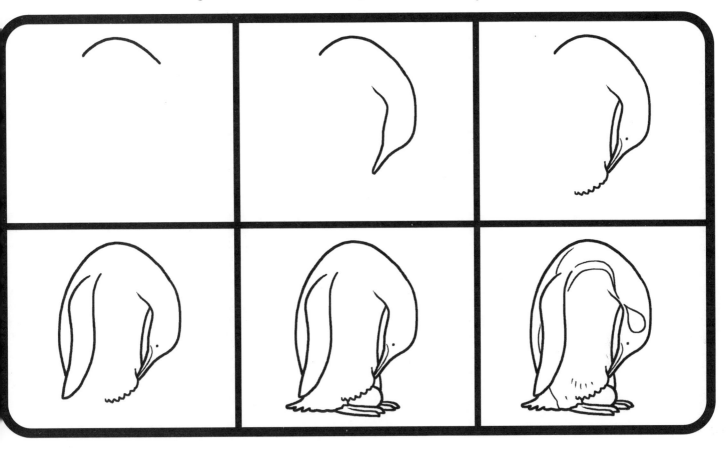

octopus

Dolphin jumping

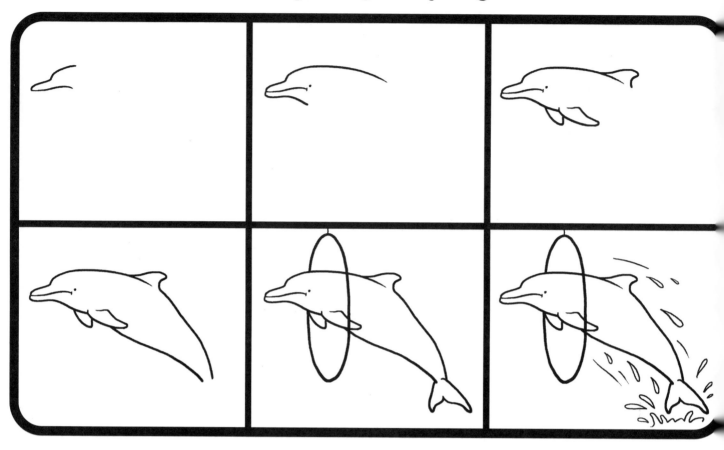

Manta Ray

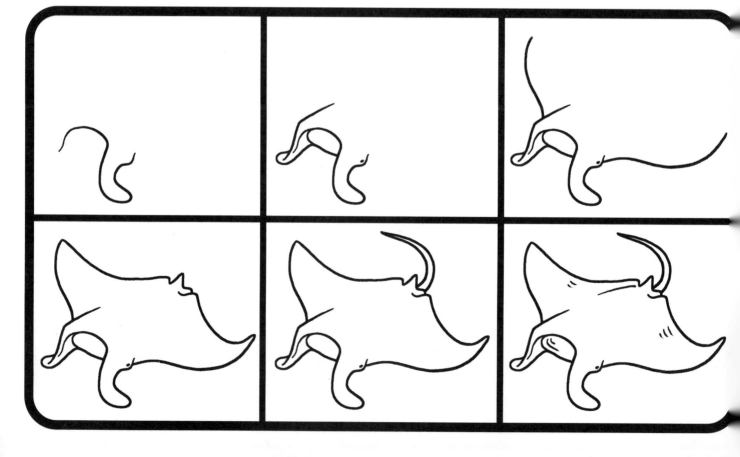

Narwhal

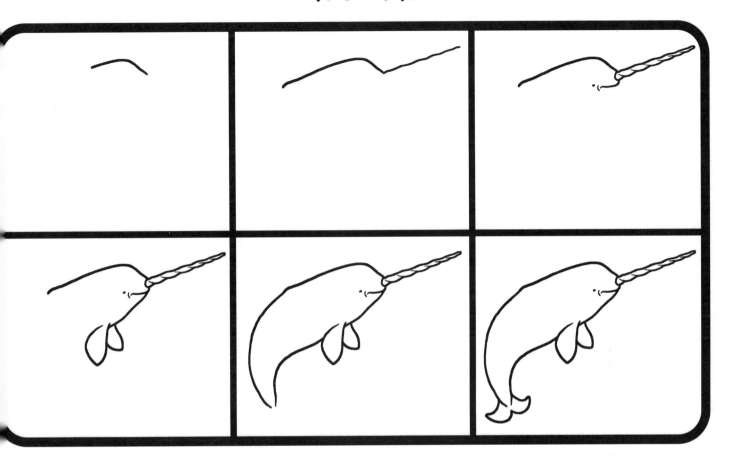

Spider crab

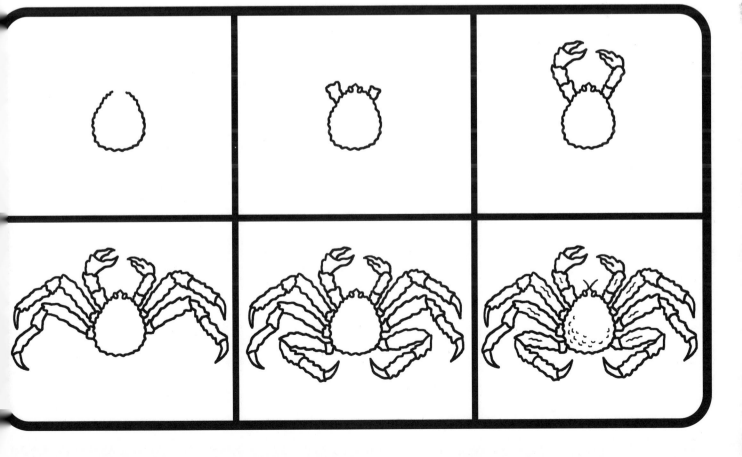

Sea Lion

Soldier fish

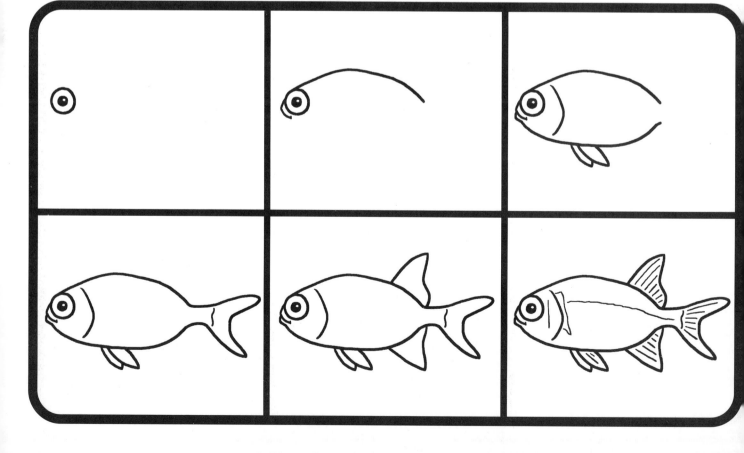

Chromis fish

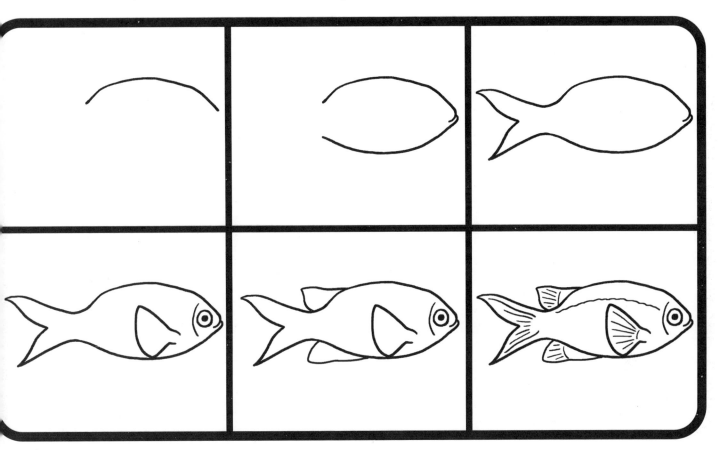

Stingray

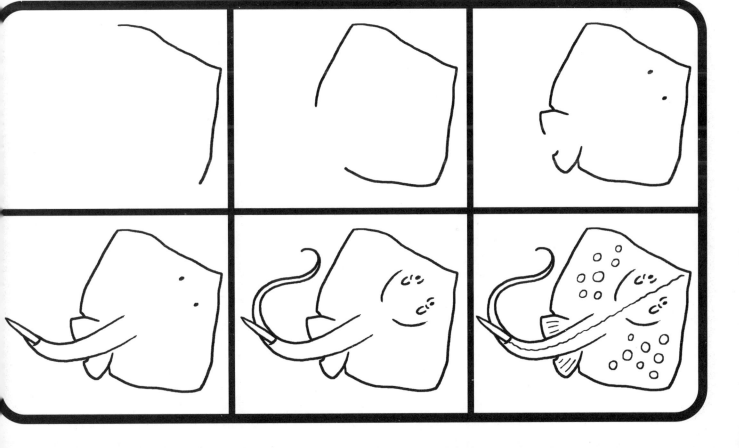

four-Eyed Butterfly fish

Baby Seal

Dusky Dolphin

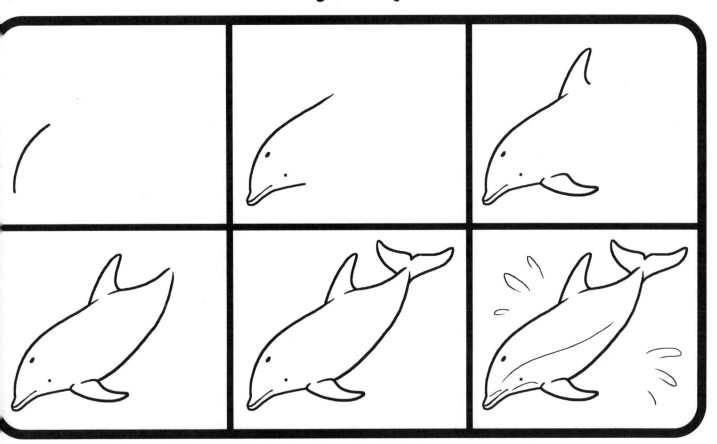

Moonfish

Anglerfish

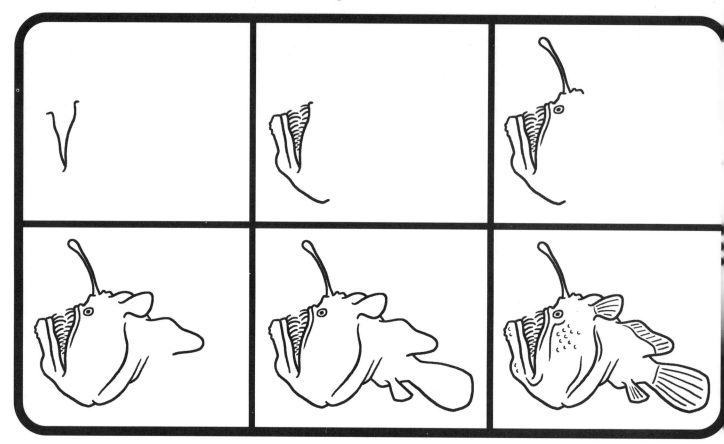

Marine Iguana

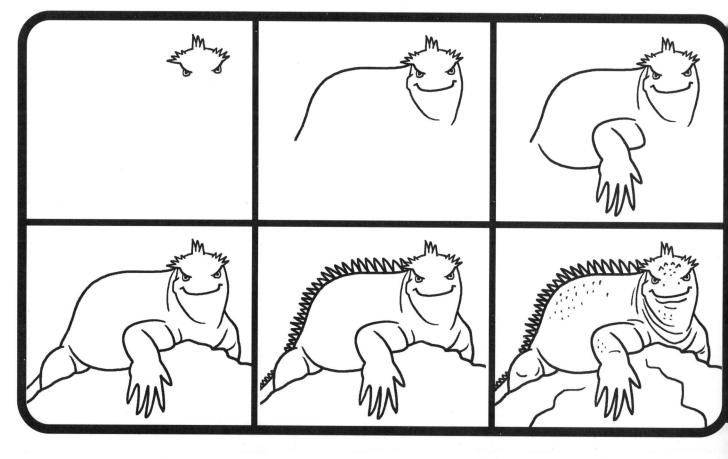

Humpback Whale

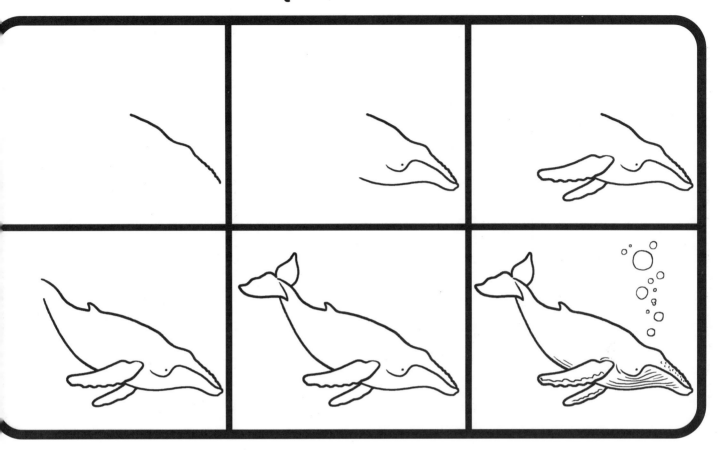

Flying Fish

Elephant Seal

Commerson's Dolphin

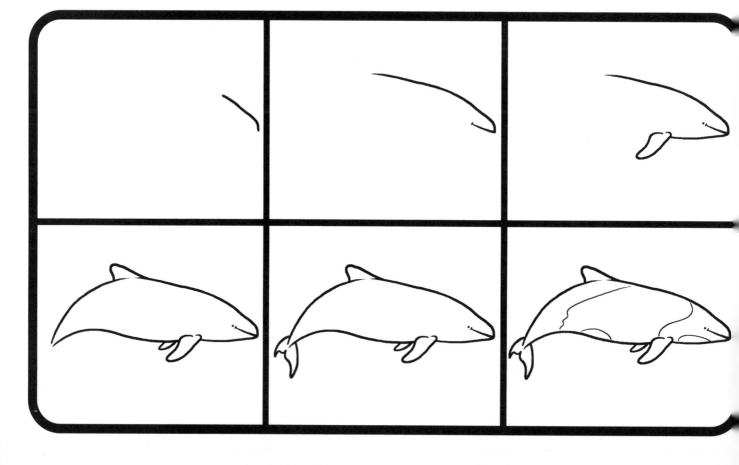

Butterfly fish

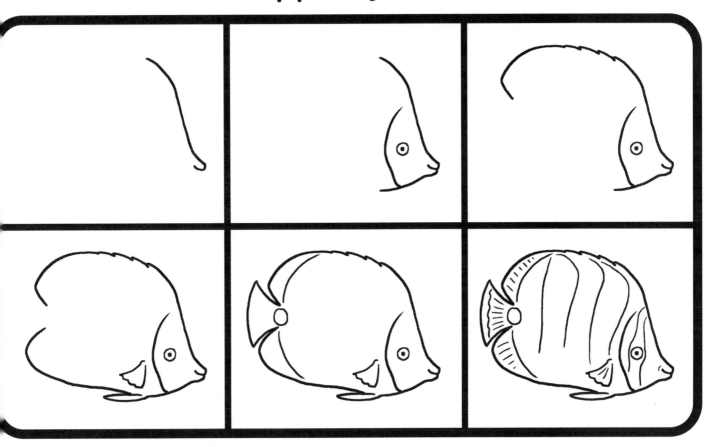

oarfish

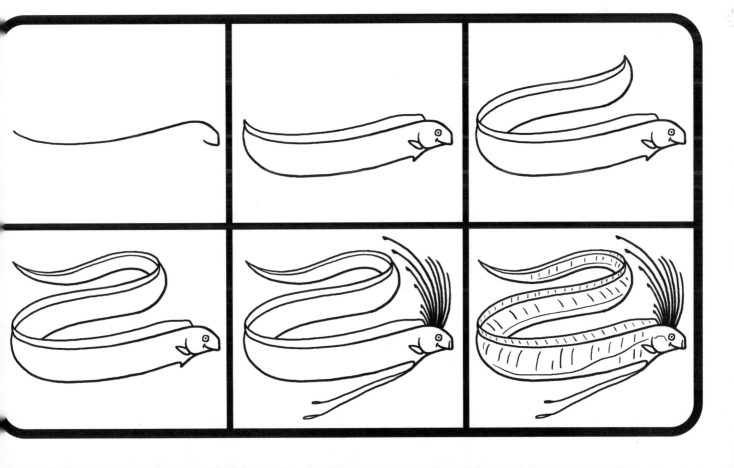

Manatee

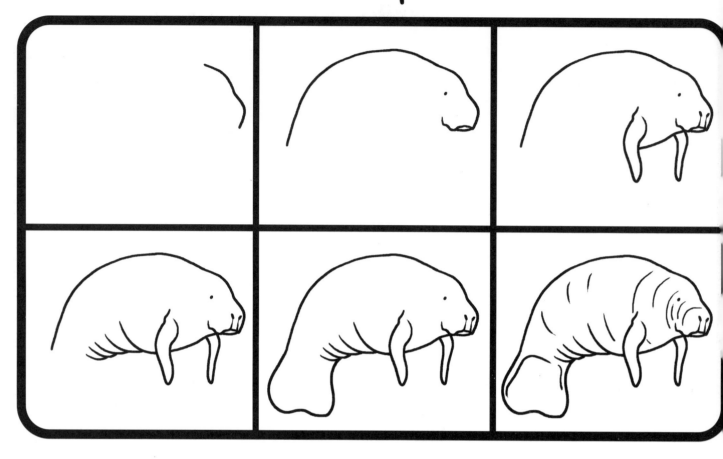

Sea Turtle

killer Whale (orca)

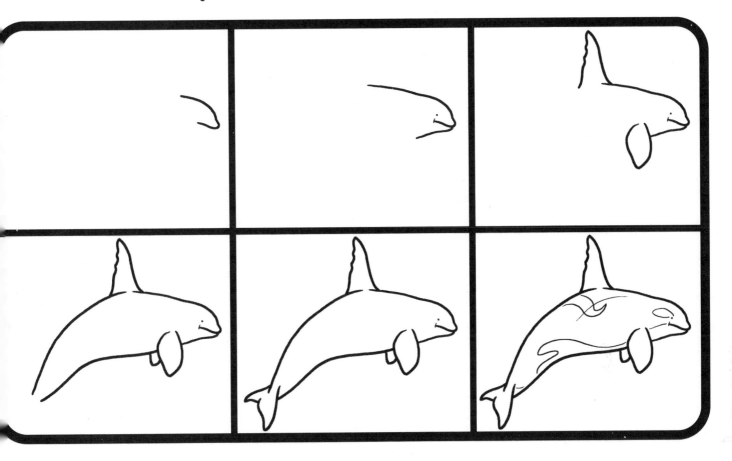

Unicorn fish

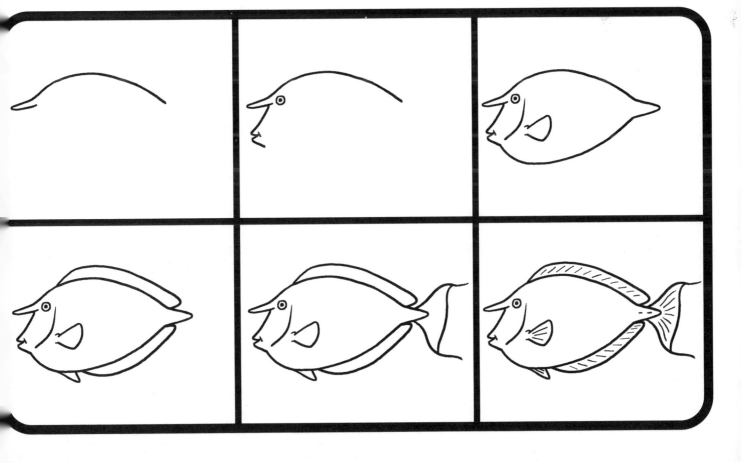

Sailfish

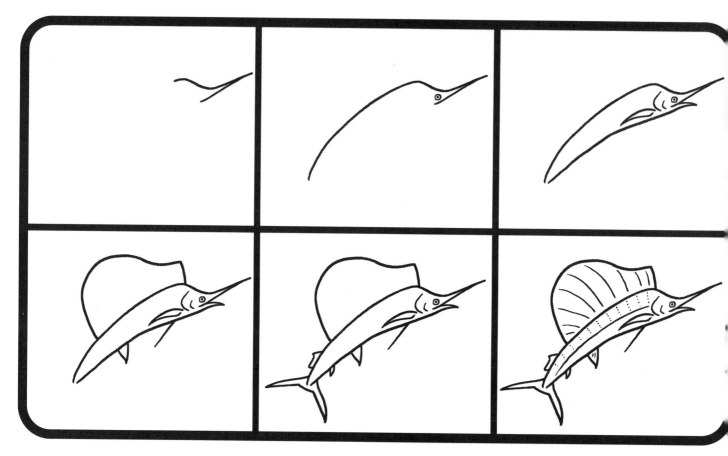

Lumpsucker

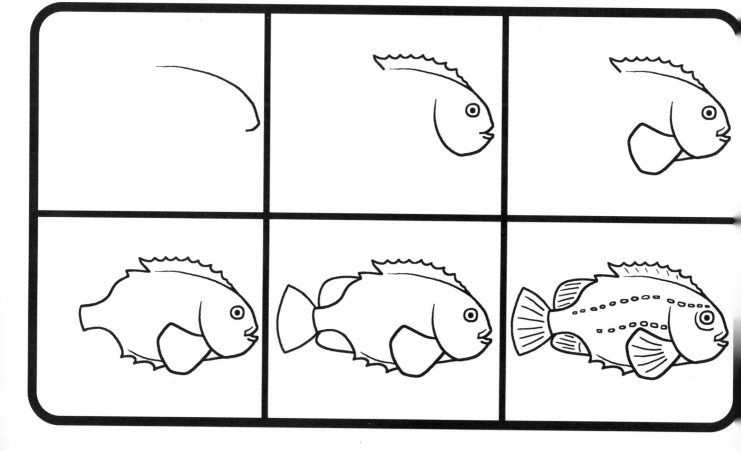

Baby Dolphin

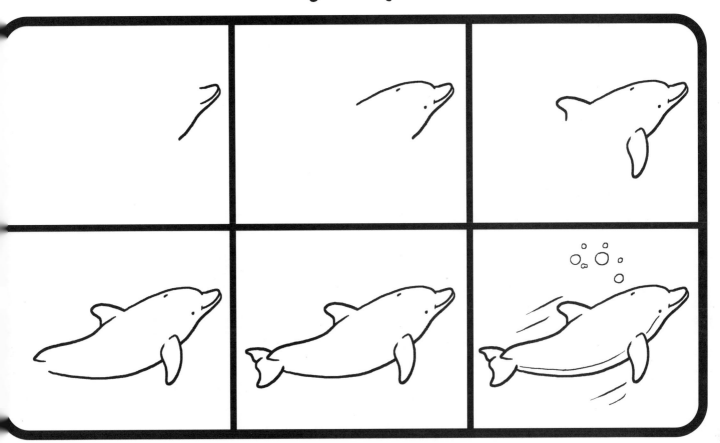

Pineapple fish

Spotted oreo

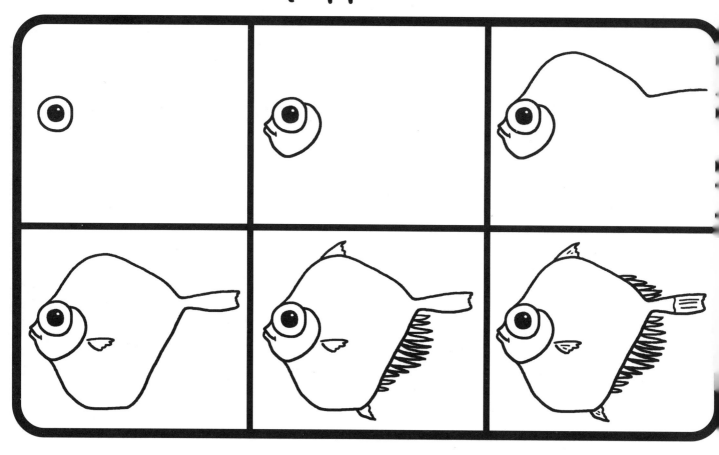

Softshell Turtle

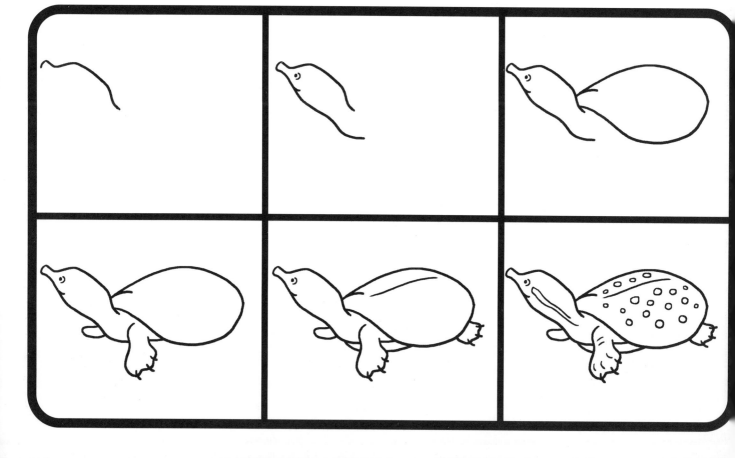

Swordfish

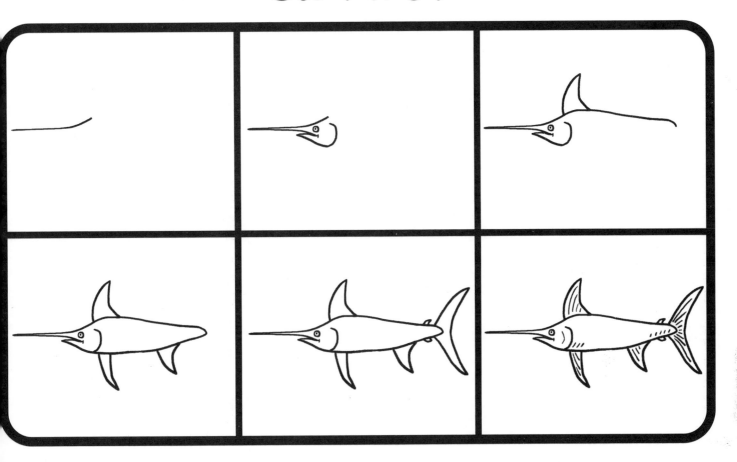

Jellyfish

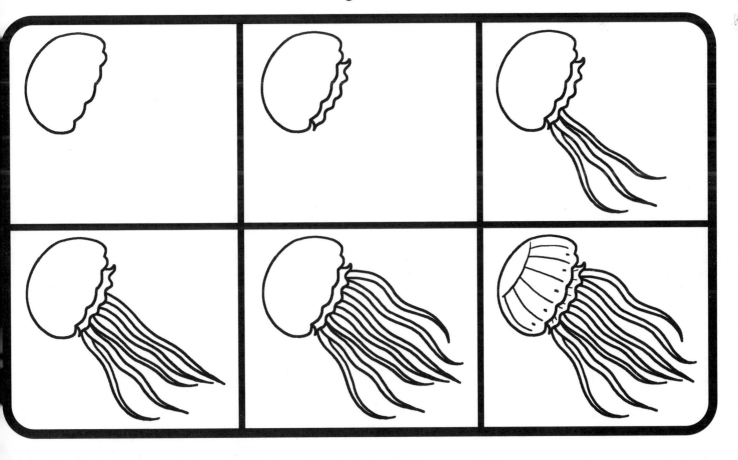

Seal

Blue-footed Booby

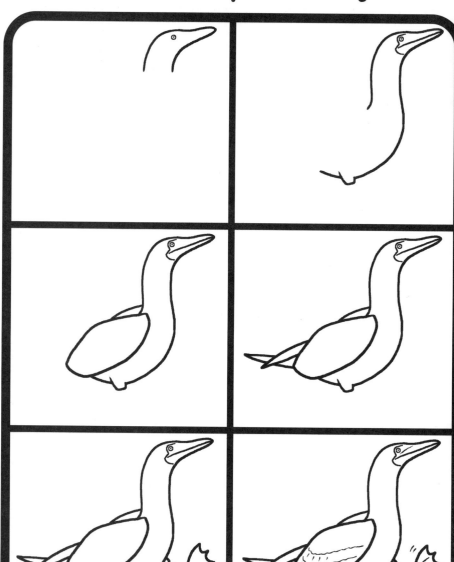

Starfish

Toadfish

cockatoo fish

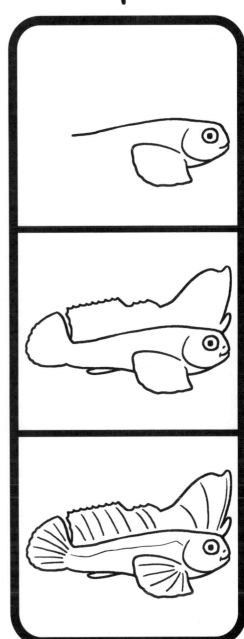

Smiling Dolphin

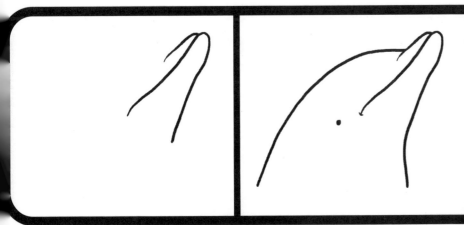

Sea Slug

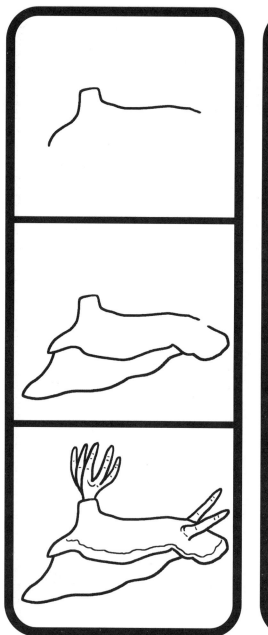

Sea otter

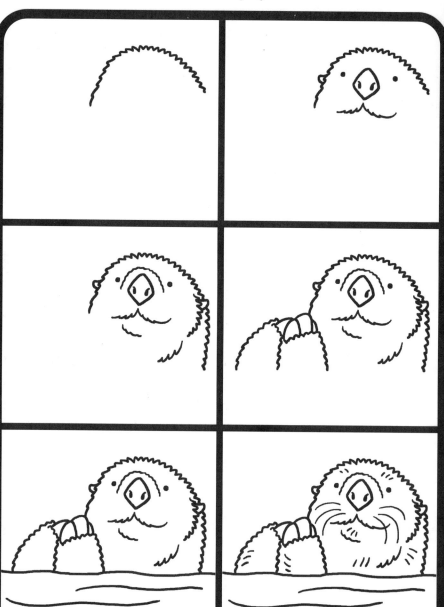

Horseshoe Crab

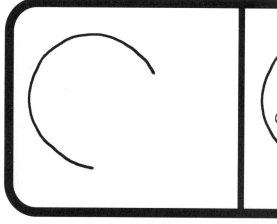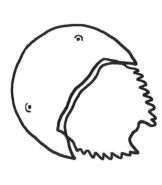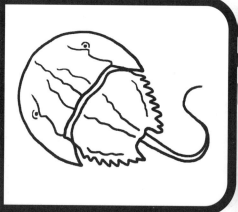

clown Knife Fish

Moon Jellyfish

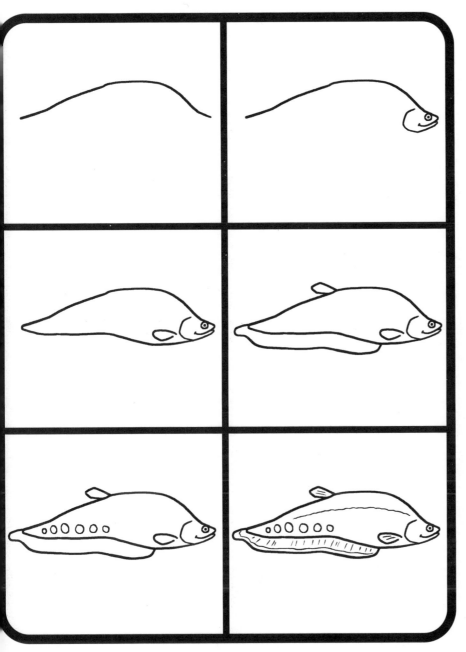

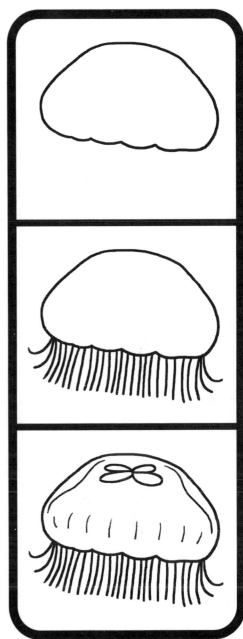

Big-Eye Thresher Shark

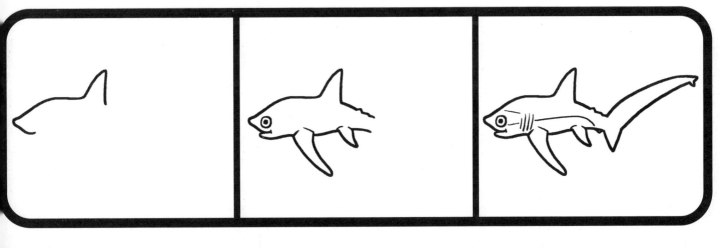

Brittle Star

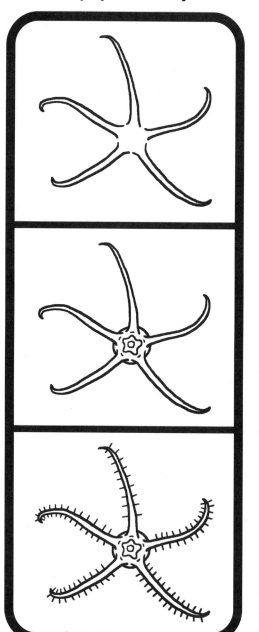

Tail-Walking Dolphin

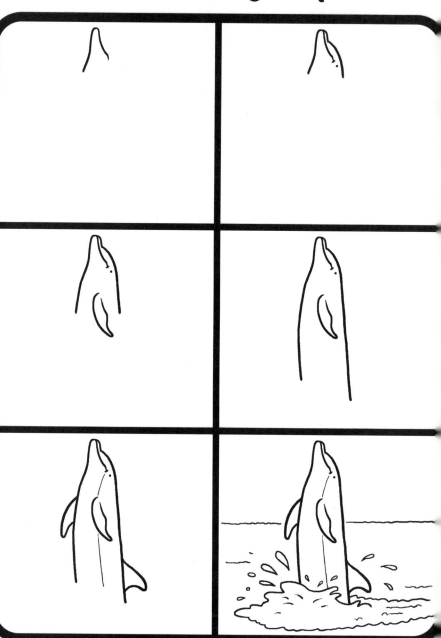

Moray Eel

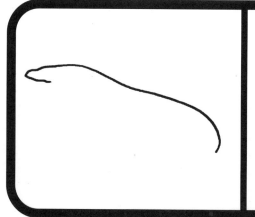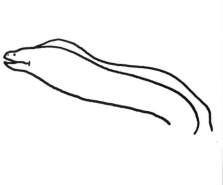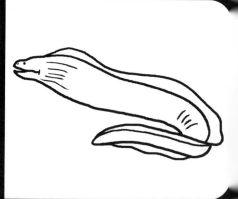

Woodland Fairy

Tooth Fairy

Water Fairy   Fairy Godmother

Starbright

Toadstool Fairy

corn fairy

fairy queen

flower fairy

Moonbeam

Christmas Fairy

Buttercup

flutter

Seaspray

Rainbow Fairy

Sunshine Fairy

Puddle

Whoosh

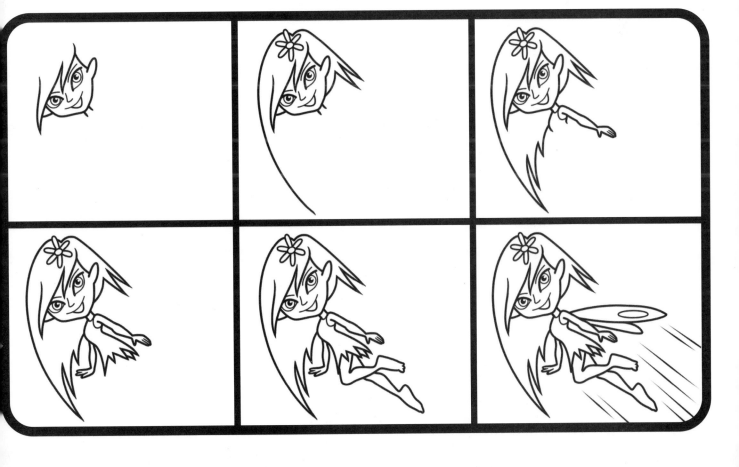

Glitter

Trixie

Velvet

Snoozy

Ruby

Daisy

Blink

Sparkle

Bubbles   Firefly

Emerald

Dewdrop

Hiccup

Breeze

Dimples

Fluffy

Blush   # Freckles

Rose

Snowdrop

Beauty

Loveheart

Twizzle

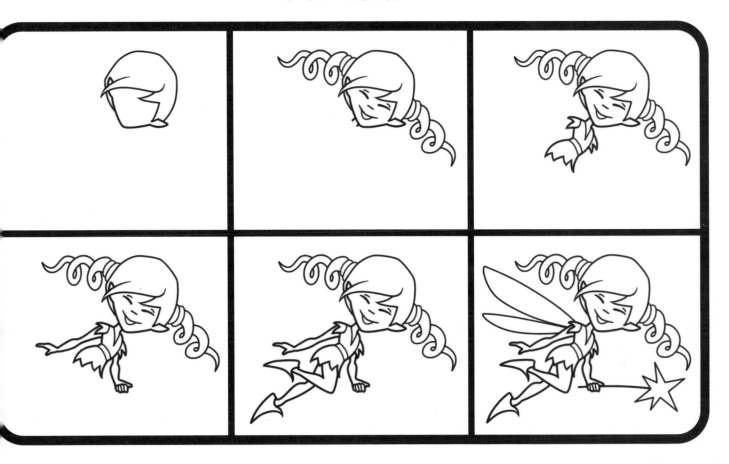

Sapphire

Dazzle

Misty

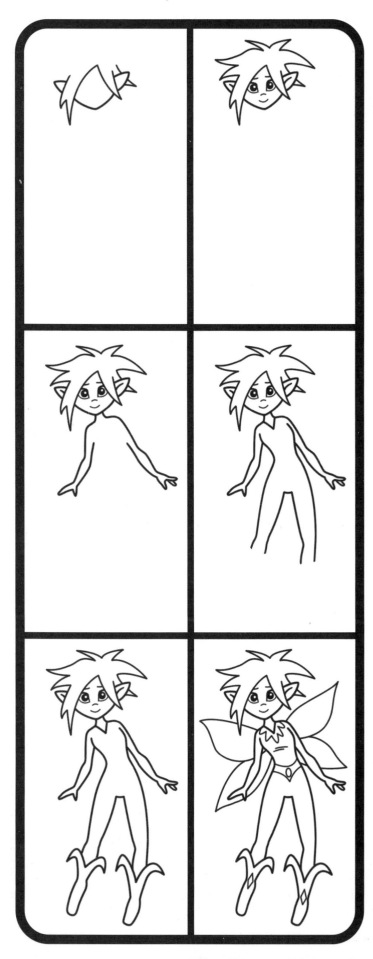

Dizzy

Lollipop

Candy

Fizz

Goldie

Charm

Snowflake

Jester

Whistler

Smudge

crystal

Tiny

Sunflower

Fidget

chuckles   cuddles

Lotus

Bumble

Shuffle   Jasmine

Raven

Alpine

Blossom   Ariel

Snuggles

Minty

Tulip

Amble

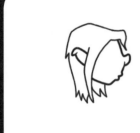

cupcake

Seashell

Prancer

Willow

flash

flora

Hazel

Pebble

frazzle

Hawkwind

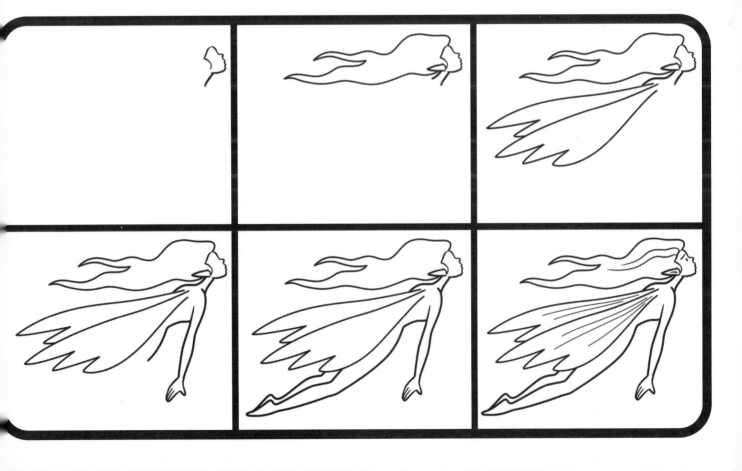

Pinky

Butterscotch

Venus

Jacaranda

Nibs

Cherry

Violet

Grace

Nixie

Coral

Andromeda

Petunia

Dragonfly

Baubles

Nightingale

Indigo

Elfin

Jiggle

Melody

Arab

Thoroughbred

Friesian

Dartmoor

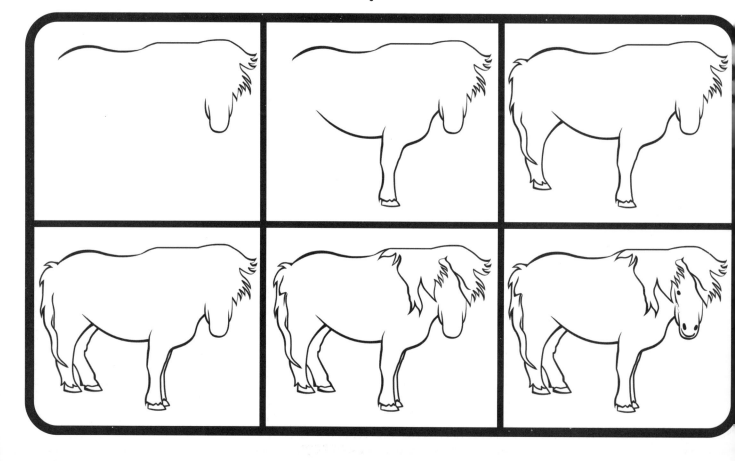

Lusitano

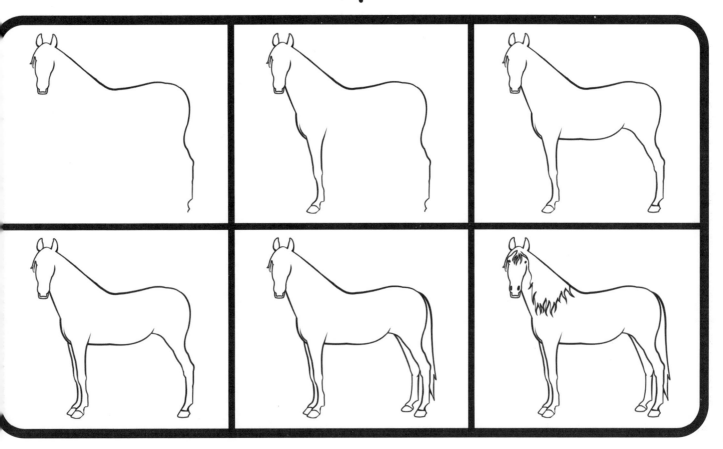

Lipizzaner

Mustang

Piebald

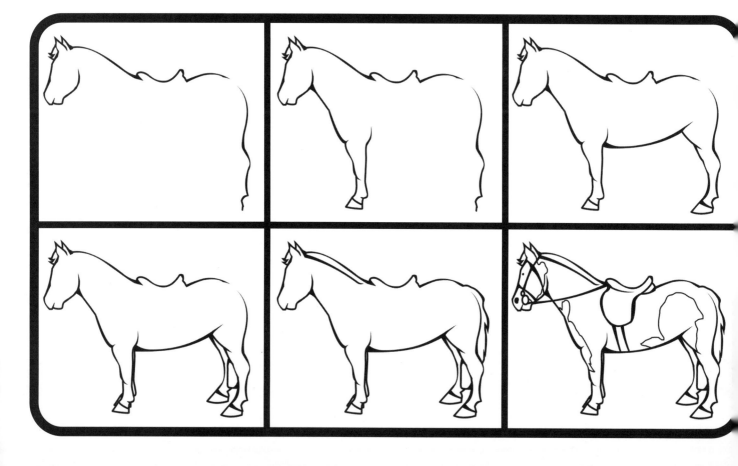

Shire

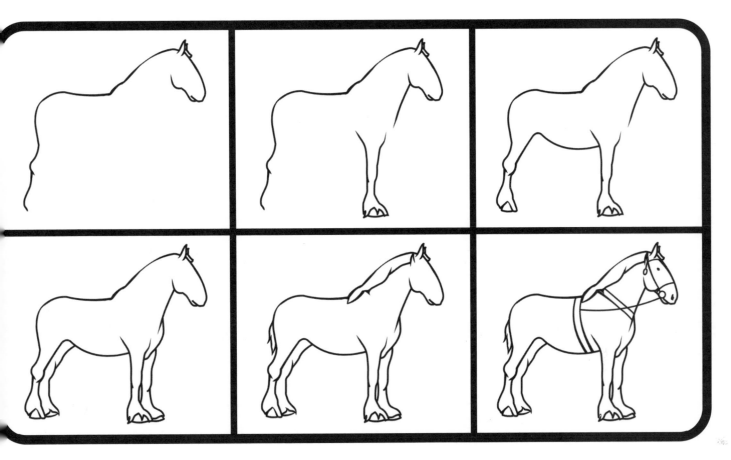

Falabella

Appaloosa

Shetland Pony

Palomino

Norwegian fjord pony

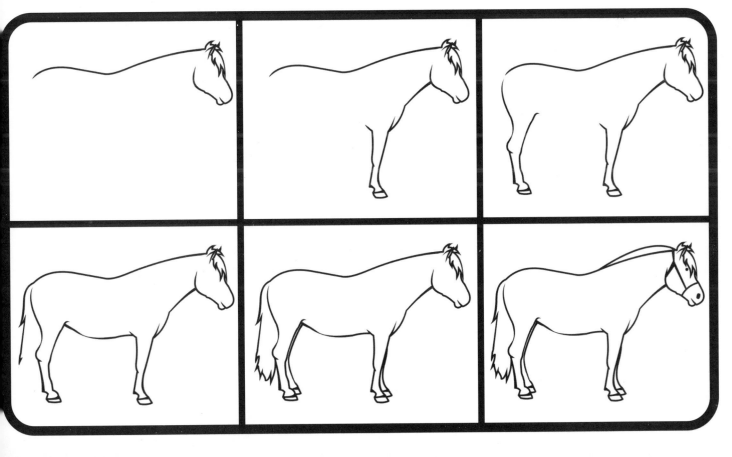

Breton

Pinto

Walking

Trotting

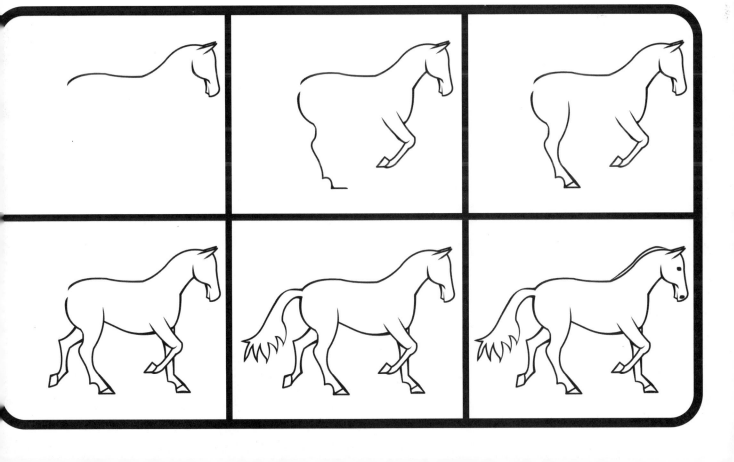

Cantering

Galloping

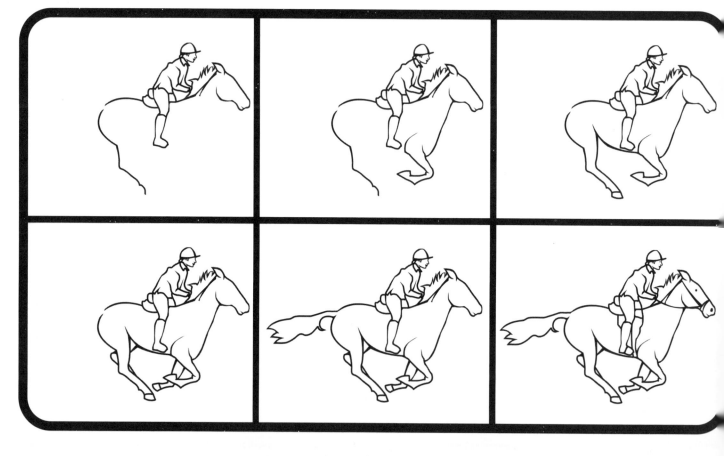

Jumping

Eating grass

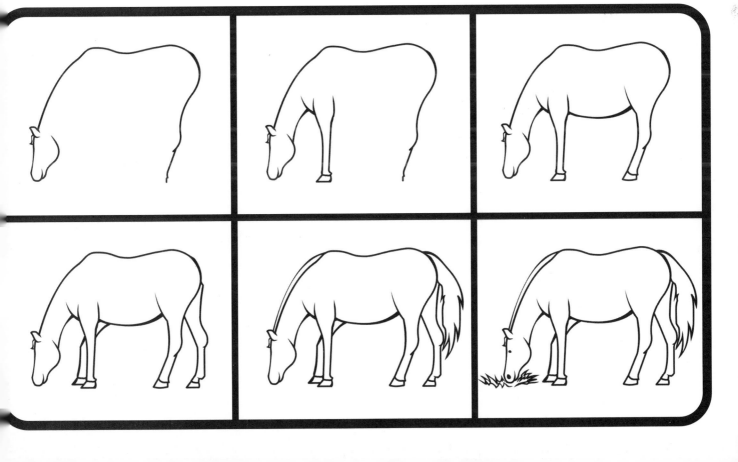

Rearing

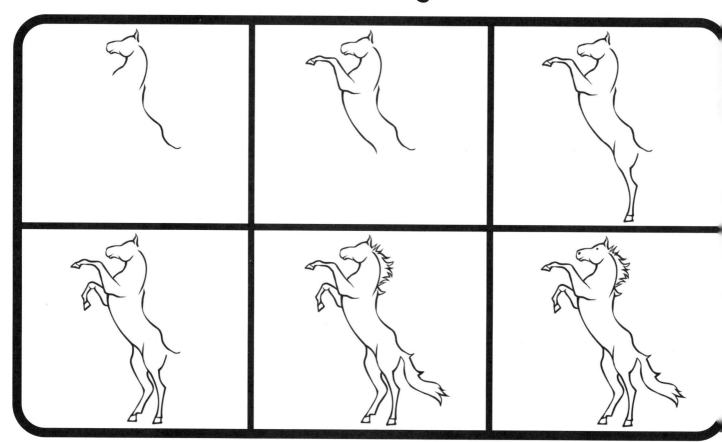

Tethered

circus horse

Whinnying

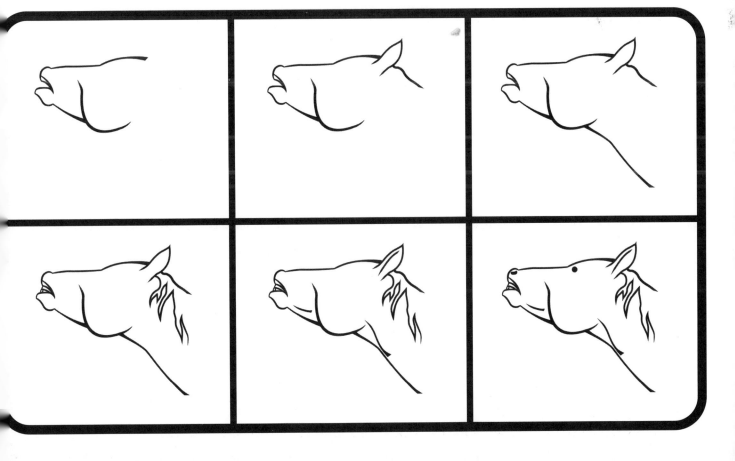

Prehistoric horse

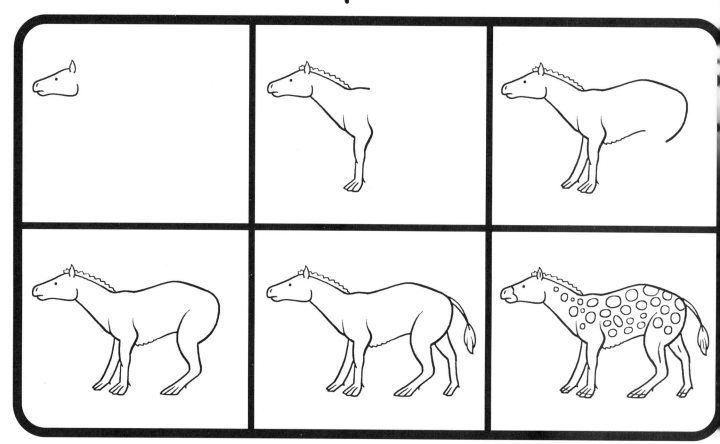

Horse and rosette

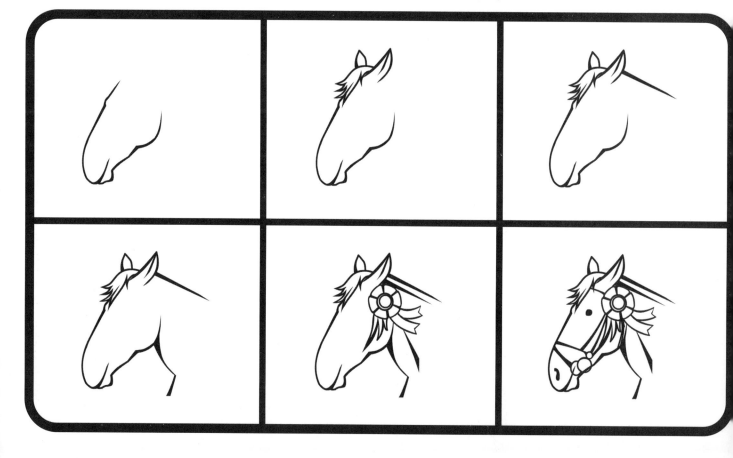

Dressage horse

Bridled horse

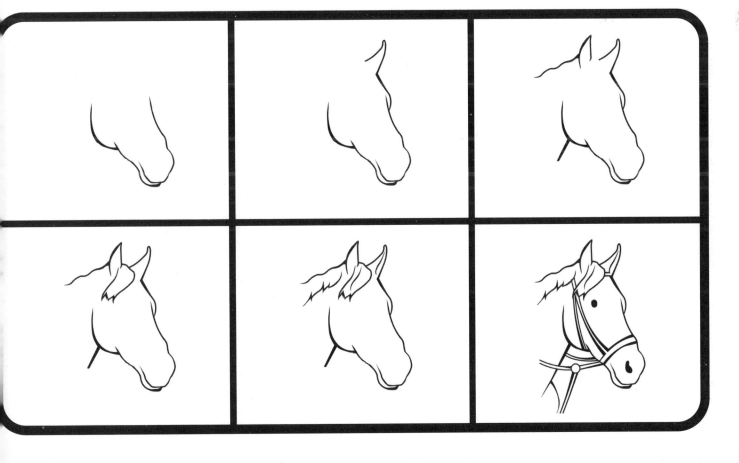

Bucking bronco with rider

Polo pony with rider

Mother and foal

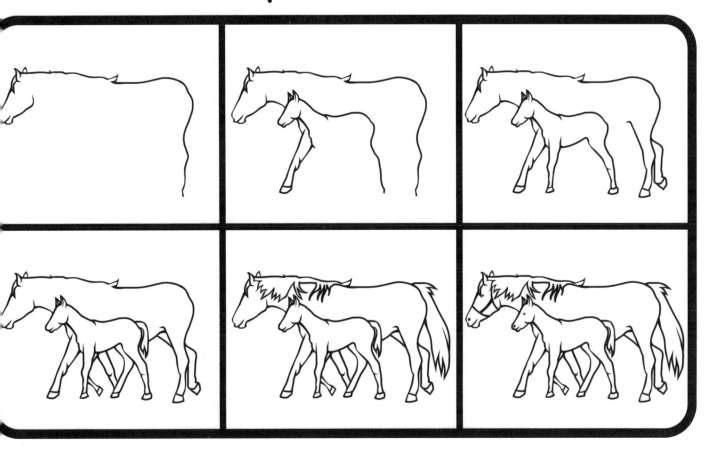

Racehorse with blinkers

Medieval tournament horse

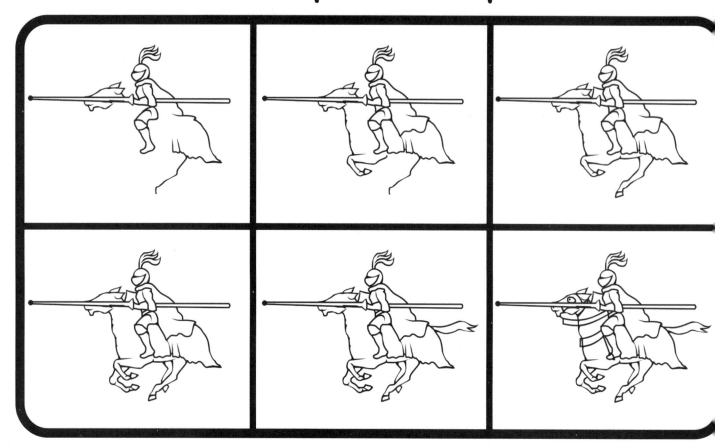

Expression; ears forward

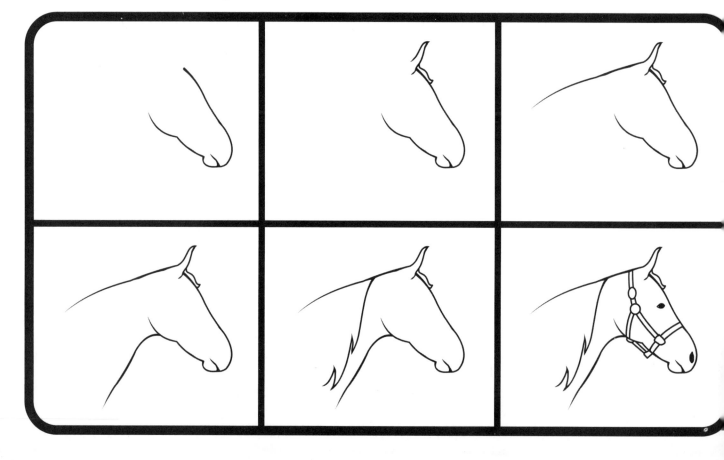

Expression; ears back

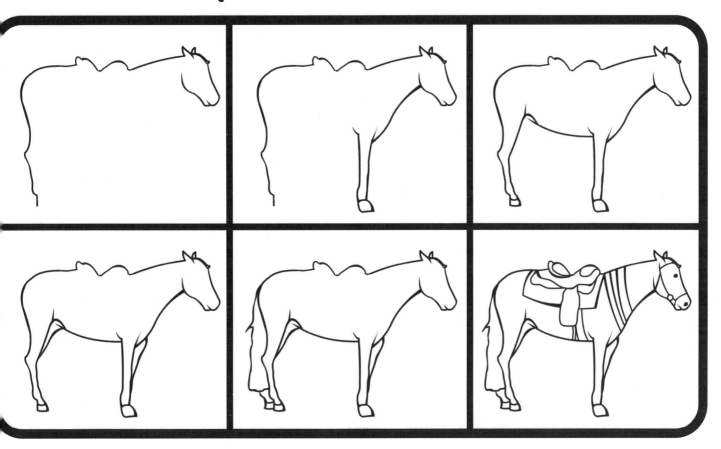

Harness racing

classical equitation

Eventing horse

Two heads nuzzling

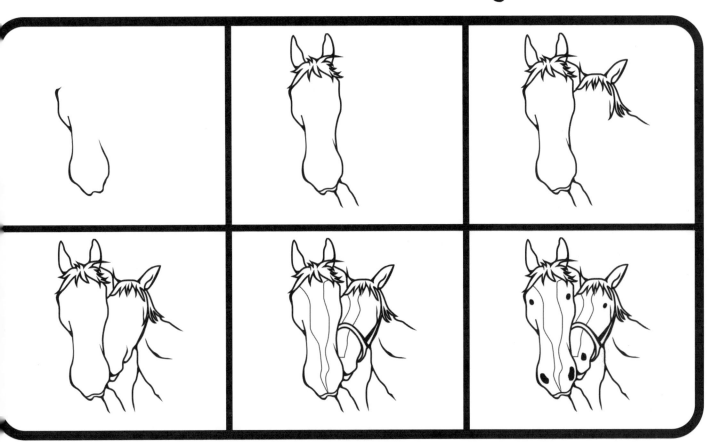

Show horse

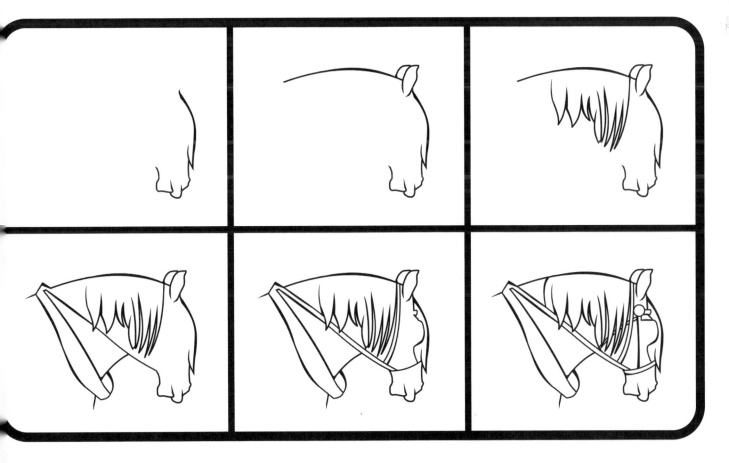

fantasy horse—unicorn head

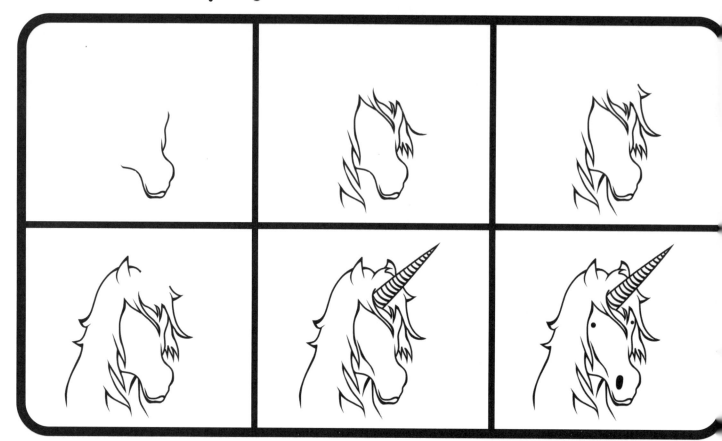

fantasy horse—Pegasus full body

fantasy horse—Pegasus head

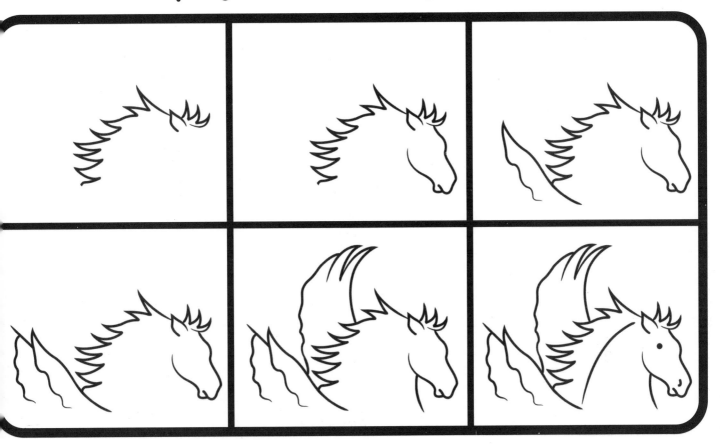

fantasy horse—unicorn full body

Mustang Close-up

Thoroughbred Close-up

Piebald pony

Eating hay

Plaited tail

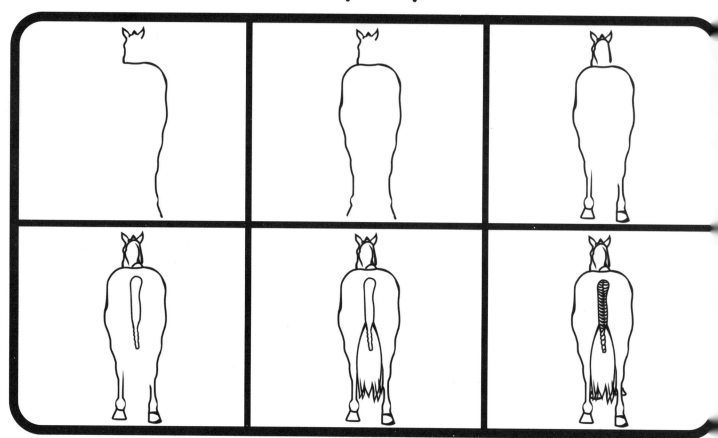

Plaited mane

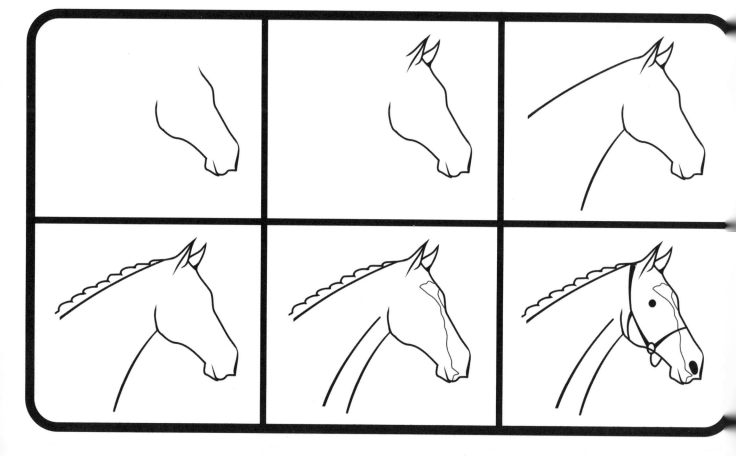

Horse in horsebox

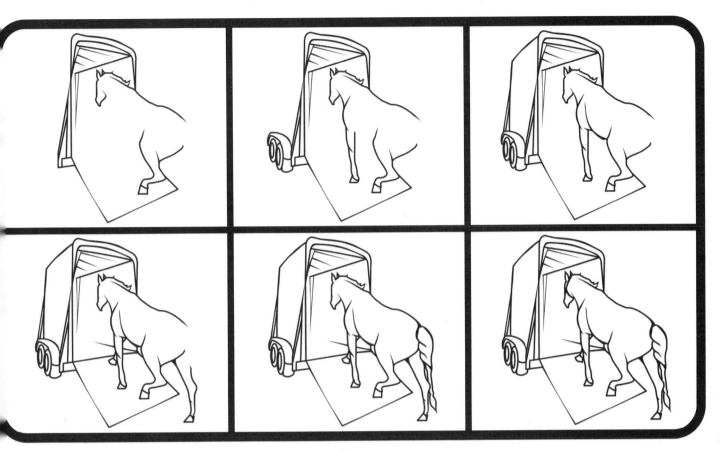

Rear view of saddle

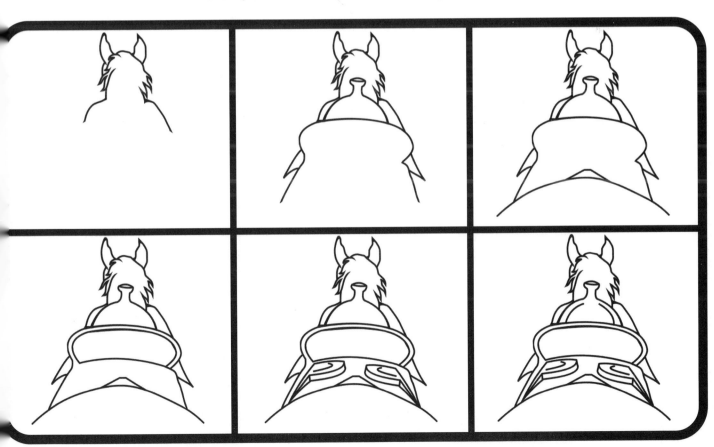

Horse lying down

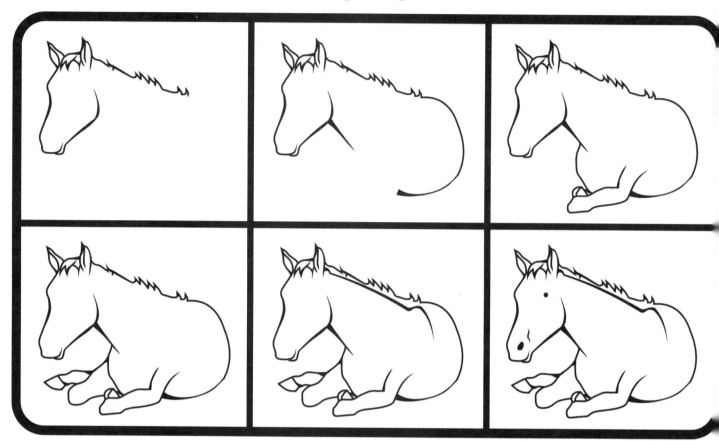

Horse rolling over

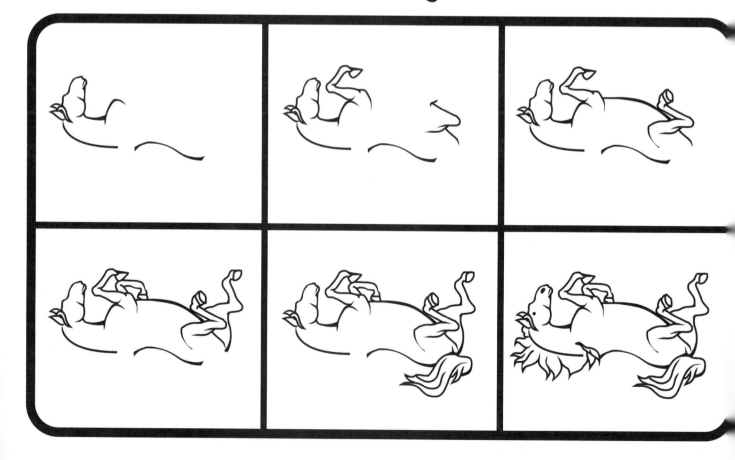

Horse pawing the ground

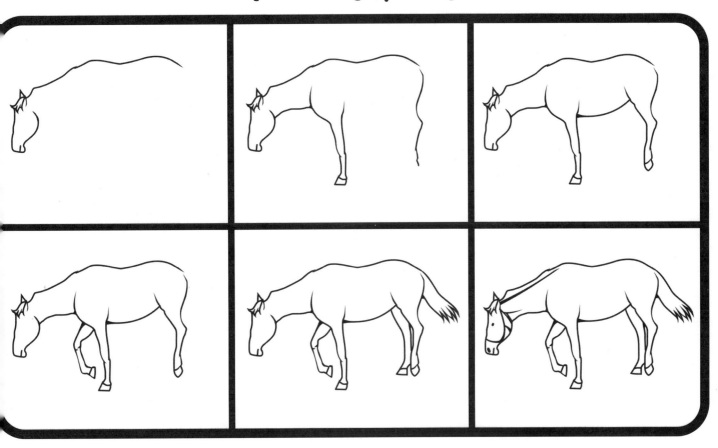

Horse with blanket

foal

Horse being re-shod

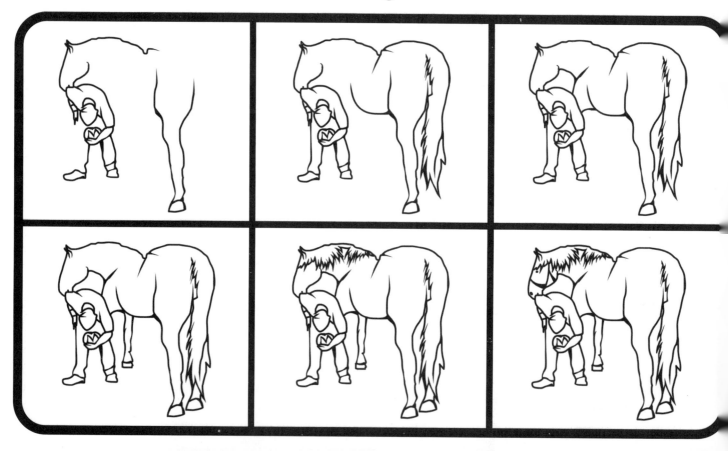

Horse led with halter

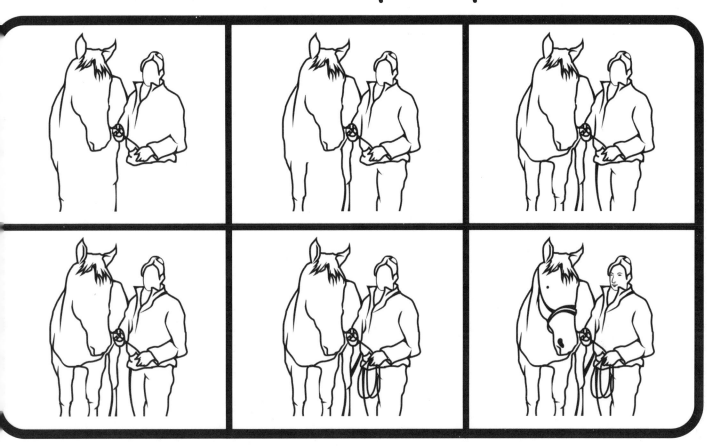

Police horse

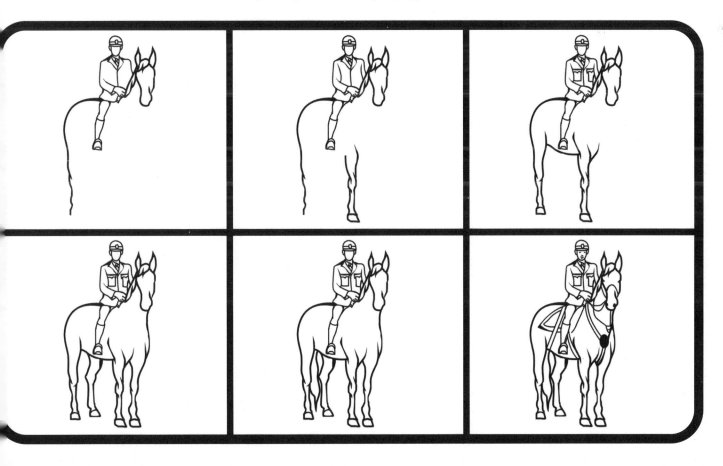

Jockey on horse

Canadian Mountie horse

Horse drinking

Horse guard

Horse with Western saddle

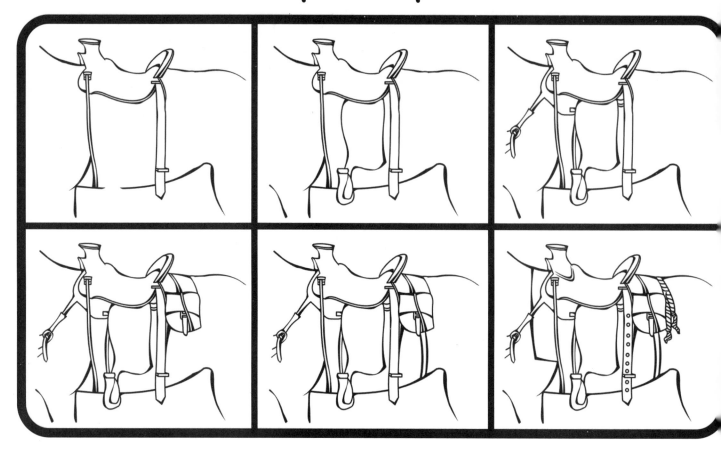

Horses with nose markings

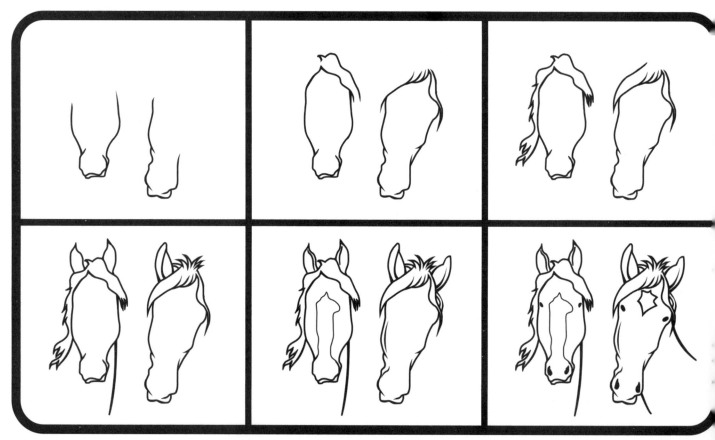

Show jumping

foal suckling mother

Play fighting

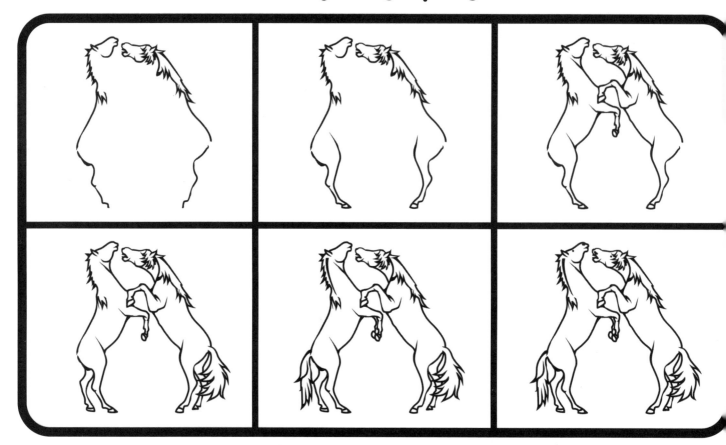

Horse jumping a countryside fence

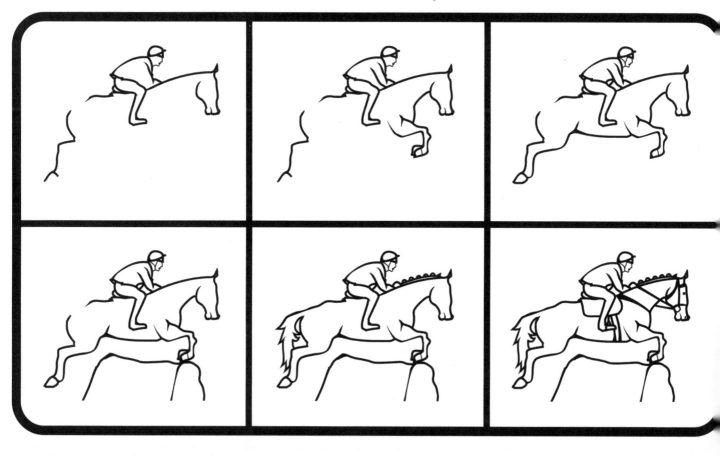

Horse trotting with rider

Buck-toothed cartoon horse

cartoon pony

cartoon seahorse

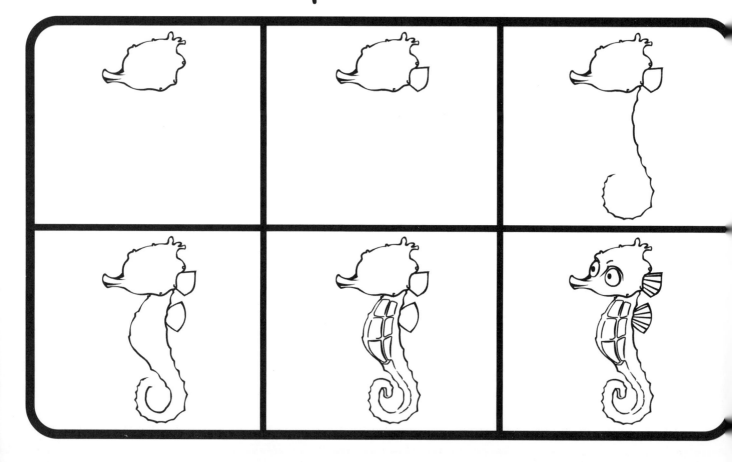

cartoon Pegasus

cartoon horse—galloping

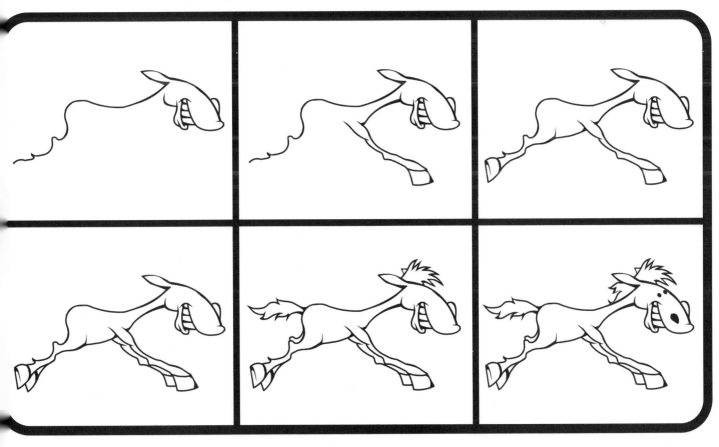

cool horse

cool pony

cartoon foal—cantering

cartoon old horse

Pop star pony

cartoon horse—flower in mouth

Horse over stable door

Horse—rear view

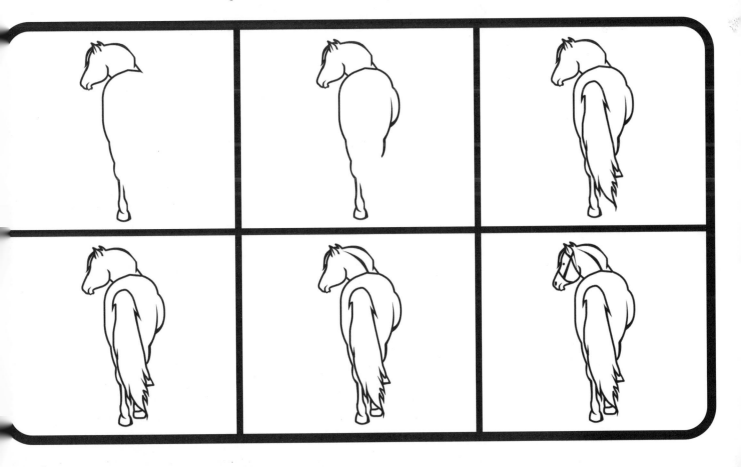

Jockey

Bucking horse

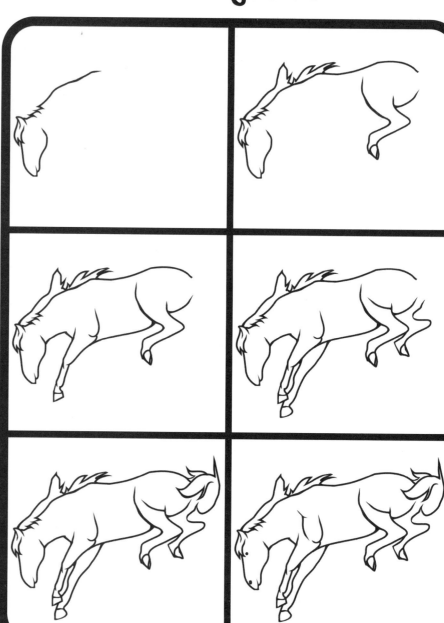

Horse Cantering through water

Horse high-trotting

Cowboy

Horse Chewing

Petting

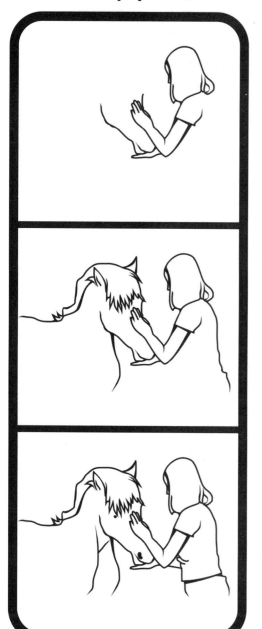

Horse and cart

Horses fighting

Wild horses

Miniature

Horse with Native American

Peering

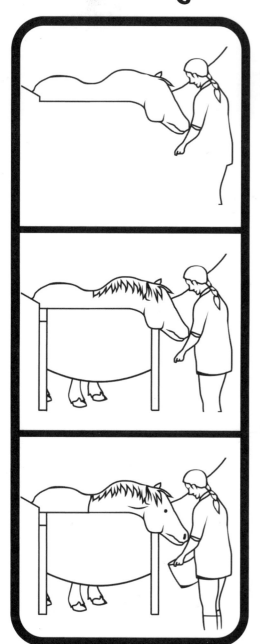

White-faced horse

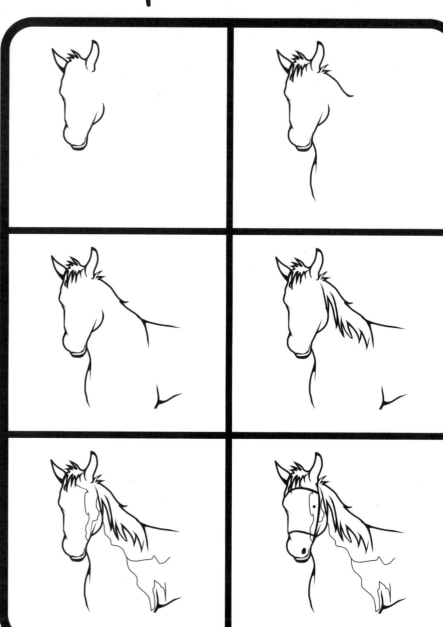

Leisure rider